COMMON SECRETARIAL MISTAKES AND HOW TO AVOID THEM

Prentice-Hall Editorial Staff

Englewood Cliffs, N.J. PRENTICE-HALL, INC.

LIBRARY OF CONGRESS
CATALOG CARD NUMBER: 63-21224

Fifteenth Printing . . . . . May, 1982

PRINTED IN THE UNITED STATES OF AMERICA

0-13-152744-4

TABLE OF CONTENTS

COMMON SECRETARIAL MISTAKES AND HOW TO AVOID THEM

The secretary's job is not one for the erratic genius; you have to be consistently good. All your hard-earned skills can be wasted if you continue to make costly mistakes that force you to do work over again, or create mayhem and confusion in your office.

Here at last, in handy booklet form, is a guide that will get you through even the toughest day without a hitch. Packed into these pages are the answers to problems that puzzle secretaries most often. And basic skills aren't the only subjects covered; a secretary must know how to dress, how to handle delicate situations where prescribed rules of etiquette govern, and how to be a watchdog over confidential material.

Even if you are a veteran, you'll find it reassuring to have information such as this at your fingertips:

How to handle cranks
How to use the comma, the hyphen
How to make office introductions
How to type a table
How to make sure your executive gets to that meeting
— and much more.

The booklet is designed to make it simple for you to find the information you want. At the same time, each subject is complete, in case you want a general brush-up. For example, you will find a thorough treatment of how to phrase and type business letters. Another section tells how to handle visitors to your office (including the ones who shouldn't be there).

Keep this helper handy. It will give you a reputation as the secretary who doesn't make mistakes.

1. WHEN THE SECRETARY ACTS AS OFFICE HOSTESS

If you tend to regard office callers as an interruption in your busy day, you are showing off your inexperience, and you are probably doing more harm than you realize. It's part of your job as a secretary to represent your executive and your company favorably to the outside world, which is where business comes from. At the same time, your executive counts on you to stand between him and unnecessary or unwanted intrusions on his time by visitors.

This section tells you how to be a gracious and helpful hostess when clients or others come to the office—and how to protect your executive's precious time from nonessential interviews.

EVERY CALLER DESERVES YOUR FULL ATTENTION. As a hostess, your duty is to make your employer's callers feel welcome, and within limits, to help them accomplish what they came for. When a caller enters your office, lay aside whatever you are doing and give him your full attention. If you are on the telephone with an important call, the visitor will usually stand back until you hang up. In any case, you always acknowledge his entrance with a smile and a nod.

Remember, you are the first person a visitor sees and so you give him his first impression of the company. If you are chewing gum in time to the typewriter, you are creating a poor image of your employer and your firm. If you are permitted to smoke at your desk, you should put out your cigarette when a visitor enters the office.

HOW TO GET A CALLER'S NAME AND BUSINESS. Every secretary has unexpected callers come into the office at one time or another. Here are some tips to remember when dealing with these people.

A caller will generally state his name and the purpose of his visit after you have greeted him. New secretaries often panic when someone says that his name is John J. Smith but won't give the reason for his call. Perhaps he says something like, "I know Mr. Jones will want to see me. We are old friends." Don't be thrown off by this approach; if Mr. Smith is a genuine friend of your employer, he won't mind stating his business.

You must be polite but firm with the Mr. Smiths who invade the office. Have ready a remark such as, "Mr. Jones is working on a very tight schedule; he told me to get this information from all callers." If your visitor still insists on admittance, suggest that he write to your employer and state the nature of his business, requesting an appointment. Should your visitor have the bad manners to persist, you must remain polite yet firm in your stand. Sometimes salesmen will test a new secretary to see if they can get around her. Once they know you will not become flustered, they are more cooperative.

Keep in mind that once a caller gets you to contact your employer, either by intercom or by entering his office, the visitor knows your boss is in. This only makes it more difficult to turn him away.

WHAT TO DO WHEN A VISITOR HAS TO WAIT. When a caller has to wait, you should offer to take his hat and coat. Let him take his coat off by himself; most men do not like to have women helping them. Offer your guest a chair and provide him with something to read and an ashtray in case he wants to smoke. You should have subscriptions to business magazines and magazines of general interest, so there is always something up to date. If there is nothing available in the line of current reading matter, offer some company literature.

Try not to let the presence of a waiting caller unnerve you. When this happens there is the danger that the visitor will realize your nervousness and seek to take advantage of the situation by luring you into conversation about your employer and the company. A nervous person tends to be more talkative to cover up a lack of poise.

Should your guest start a conversation, you are obliged to be courteous and reply. This does not mean you are at liberty to discuss your boss or your work. If your guest becomes inquisitive about matters you know are not for general discussion, be noncommittal; play dumb or tactfully change the subject.

With a little practice you will find it very easy to field leading questions and turn them into pleasant conversation without revealing confidential information. For example, a caller might ask, "I hear you're handling the Adams contract. How is it coming along?" Your reply might be, "I really don't know. I haven't been in contact with it. Our new building will be going up soon, though; would you like to see a drawing of what it will look like?"

WHAT TO SAY WHEN YOUR EMPLOYER IS OUT. Through carelessness, you can give the false impression that your executive is avoiding a particular visitor. You must be very careful in using the stock expressions, "He's in conference," or "He just left," even if you are telling the truth. These have become the stereotyped answers for secretaries who are trying to get rid of unwanted callers. When your employer is really out of his office, be tactful and sincere when you explain the circumstances to the caller. Give him as much detail as possible but don't overdo it. If your boss is in conference, you might say, "Mr. Jones was called for a conference with the president about fifteen minutes ago." If the caller had an appointment, you will undoubtedly add that the conference was unscheduled and convey your employer's personal apologies.

HOW TO TURN PEOPLE AWAY. Perhaps the most difficult problem a beginner faces is turning away visitors her employer doesn't want to see. She must be polite and convey a feeling of regret, yet remain firm if the caller should insist on being admitted.

Salesmen. If your employer has no need for something a salesman is offering, be frank and explain this to the salesman. A vague turndown—"He's in conference"—only encourages a salesman to try again another time, which wastes more of his time, and yours. You might offer to take his card, in case a future need should arise.

Solicitors for charity. No doubt your employer makes a number of charitable contributions each year, but this will not deter other charities from trying to get on his list. As with salesmen, your best approach is an honest answer. Simply explain, "Mr. Jones is already committed to several charities for the coming year and he cannot possibly take on any more." If a solicitor is especially insistent, suggest that he or she send your employer a letter.

Your employer's associates. Many executives today believe in an open door policy where company associates are concerned. Even though your employer follows this practice, the day arrives when he doesn't want to be disturbed by ANYONE. Fellow workers will usually understand when you explain he simply can't see them; give the reason, if it isn't confidential. If an associate says it is an emergency, try to find out what the problem is before you interrupt your executive.

Good customers and friends. Your executive may have friends, or good customers or clients, who are prone to drop in on him for social visits. On days when he is "snowed under," he may give you instructions such as these: "Ed Brown usually comes by on Thursday afternoon, but I just can't spare the time today to talk to him. Apologize for me when he comes, will you?" When Mr. Brown does arrive, simply explain the situation to him and convey your executive's apologies in a sincere tone. But don't be tentative; it should be clear that there is a good reason, and that the caller is not being given the brush-off, as though he were unwelcome.

► **Note.** Never take it upon yourself to turn away a caller of this kind on your own initiative; do so only if your executive instructs you to.

Cranks. Cranks are chronic complainers. They have all sorts of trivial problems that will take up your employer's time, if they can get past you. Their demands are unreasonable and generally the problem cannot be solved by your executive anyway. This is by far the most trying group you will have to handle. You must be careful not to let them draw you into an argument on why they can't be admitted. At the same time you must make if perfectly clear that your employer doesn't wish to discuss their problems now or in the future. If this isn't impressed into their minds, they will keep coming back to annoy you.

Cranks are usually noted for their lack of manners, which makes it easier for you to come right to the point. Just say "Mr. Jones is a very busy man and has left instructions that he is not to be disturbed for interviews of this nature." Should a crank go so far as to make a scene, you will have to call on another executive to help you out, but do not call on your boss. Try to get one of his associates.

WHEN YOUR EMPLOYER'S FAMILY COMES TO CALL. Sooner or later your office door will open, a woman will enter and say, "Hello, I am Mrs. Jones. Will you please tell my husband I'm here?" Whether you have been expecting her or not, as a beginner you may feel nervous about your first contact with your employer's wife. Relax and treat her as you would any other caller. Take her coat and offer her a chair and then inform your employer of her arrival. He will generally take it from there.

Sometimes your employer will be busy and won't be able to see her right away. Don't panic when this occurs. Business wives know their husbands cannot always drop everything when they arrive, so you needn't go into long apologies if Mr. Jones isn't instantly available. Simply explain the situation and then offer her something to read or a cup of coffee if you have it available. You may just pass the time with a pleasant chat if you aren't particularly busy. Take your cue from her. If she is content to sit and read, let her. If she wants to talk, be a good listener.

► **Hint.** You might find it a good idea to keep a game or puzzle on hand in case the children come along too. If there is nothing to occupy their little minds, they will spend the time exploring files and any other easily accessible drawers.

HOW TO INTERRUPT YOUR BOSS WHEN HE HAS A VISITOR. Sometimes it becomes necessary for you to contact your employer while he has a visitor in his office. Your course of action will be determined by the circumstances.

Your boss wants to get rid of a visitor. Set up a signal with your employer to cover this problem. A quick buzz or two over the intercom will do. Then you knock quietly on his office door, go in and deliver a pre-arranged message. It may be a simple phrase: "Your California call is ready now, Mr. Jones," or "Mr. Adams has arrived." Either of these informs the visitor that your employer is a busy man.

An urgent private message arrives for your employer. Don't let emergencies throw you off balance. If the message isn't a written one, take a minute to type it out, and then put it in a plain envelope. This gives your employer something to put it back in, and saves him the embarrassment of trying to keep it from the eyes of his caller. Knock lightly on the door and deliver the message with an "Excuse me but this just arrived for you, Mr. Jones, and it is marked 'Urgent'."

Your employer or his visitor is wanted on the telephone. Excuse yourself and deliver the information to the party concerned. Your employer may offer his phone to the visitor, should the call be for him.

SUMMARY. Eight points to remember when you are the office hostess:

1. Receive every caller as if he were a guest in your own home.
2. The two most important words for the receptionist are *tact* and *courtesy*.
3. Be relaxed and natural, and so will your visitors.
4. Never argue or allow yourself to be provoked by a rude caller.
5. Don't engage in conversation on private business matters with callers.
6. Be sincere and express regret when you have to turn someone away.
7. Remain polite but firm in turning away unwelcome visitors. Never lose your composure, even when faced with an ill-mannered visitor.
8. Remember that everything you do or say reflects on your employer. Be sure you are a credit to him.

2. ETIQUETTE AND PERSONAL RELATIONS IN THE OFFICE

Too many secretaries make the mistake of thinking that etiquette is something you study before attending a formal dinner. Follow the example of successful secretaries who know better. They realize that etiquette is important in business, too; it is a part of every working day. Proper and pleasant personal relations are very much a part of your job—and may be a difficult part, if you haven't had much experience. In this section you'll find tips that will give you confidence in handling the "diplomatic" side of your responsibilities as a secretary.

THE IMPORTANCE OF ETIQUETTE TO YOU AND YOUR EXECUTIVE. A secretary is her executive's representative; if she "bucks the system," or violates company protocol, it reflects poorly on him. There is a definite sense of propriety in even the smallest business office. One important reason is that people work well together only if they treat each other with courtesy and respect. A secretary who violates the principles of office etiquette, or is universally disliked or forever embroiled in office feuds, cannot expect to remain a secretary for long. Such behavior can only result in a breakdown of communications with other offices, which hurts the executive as well as the secretary.

DEALING WITH THE UPPER ECHELON. Companies, like armies, have chains of command, which you are expected to honor. This doesn't mean you kowtow to your executive or others above you, or demean yourself in any way. Nor is there any reason to get the shakes when a high company official comes into the office. But you are expected to show respect for the position that responsible people hold and to refrain from acting with authority that you don't have.

The most important rule for you to remember is—respect rank within your company. The quickest way to ruin your career as a secretary is to go over your employer's head. When your boss refuses your request for a day off, don't go to the vice-president with a tale of woe. Stop and think. Perhaps the time you want is right in the middle of a busy period when your employer needs you at the office. Never dismiss your employer's judgment lightly. Remember, his superior is more likely to see his side of the issue, rather than yours. Learn to work through channels and you will find your path a lot smoother.

UNDERSTAND THE EMOTIONAL STRAINS ON YOUR SUPERVISORS. The higher an executive goes in an organization, the more people he is responsible for, and the bigger the decisions he has to make. If your executive is sometimes grouchy or unfriendly, and neglects to say "Good Morning" or "Thank You," don't take offense. A professional secretary understands these moods and recognizes them as passing outbursts resulting from too many worries at one time.

Consider this fact, too: an executive can't tell his troubles around the office, and he is seldom free to reflect dissatisfaction to his colleagues. As his secretary, you're around to hear his grumbling. But part of your job is to act as a shock absorber during these periods. Don't take your employer's actions personally and make matters worse by engaging in petty retaliations. After all, these are the times when he is surrounded by grim faces; try to make yours the ray of sunshine that melts the chip off his shoulder.

BE PREPARED TO WORK UNDER SOMEONE YOUNGER THAN YOURSELF. It is quite possible that you work for someone younger than yourself, especially if you are beginning your secretarial career later in life. You should feel neither resentment nor uneasiness at having a young supervisor. If your boss is unusually young, then he must be an exceptional man to hold such a position. Just try to treat him as the capable person he is and forget the age factor; he will return the compliment.

DON'T RESENT TAKING ORDERS FROM A WOMAN. Beginners have usually been subjected, at one time or another in their lives, to the old wives' tales about female bosses. They go something like this: "Women are catty. They have pets. You have to constantly flatter their vanity." The list is almost endless.

Of course, a woman is not always a perfect boss, but then how many of her male counterparts are absolute angels? Expect your female supervisor to be as good as her male colleagues and you will not be disappointed, and neither will she. You can expect to enjoy working for a woman just as much as for a man, if you approach the relationship with an open mind.

GETTING ALONG WITH A "DIFFICULT" EXECUTIVE. If you feel that your executive is difficult to work for, you may be right—but even if you are, the problem is essentially yours, and not his. Whatever the reason for it, you should not let such a situation drag on without trying to iron it out. You can't do your best work when you are resentful; and your executive certainly doesn't want this kind of climate in his office.

If the problem seems to be a small thing that keeps cropping up, you can probably work it out by *discussing* it with him (not accusing him). For example, he might not realize that you weren't trained for a special kind of assignment you are often asked to do. Or he may be unaware of a problem you are having with certain equipment, or with another department.

If the problem is one that, after careful consideration, you decide cannot be ironed out, then it may be advisable to request a transfer to another office. Under no circumstances should you vent your personal feelings about a superior to his face and create an unpleasant situation you will inevitably regret.

BE PREPARED TO ACCEPT CRITICISM. If you become upset whenever your executive points out an error in your work, you are guilty of a typical beginner's mistake. The most important thing to remember in accepting criticism is this; *never* take it personally. Your executive is criticizing your work, not your personality or your upbringing. Actually, he is pointing out stumbling blocks that could keep you from doing your best work—and he wants you to learn and grow.

If your executive never offers constructive criticism, you should ask him for a conference now and then to find out what he thinks of your performance on the job. You have a right to know how you are doing, and where he thinks you might improve. In the absence of this kind of mutual understanding, you could find yourself transferred one day and never know exactly why (true, your executive would be at fault if this were to happen, but that doesn't help).

Should you exchange gifts with your employer? You are not expected to give your employer a gift at holidays, birthdays, or the like. You will only embarrass him and yourself if you give him a present when he has not planned one for you—especially if you have picked an expensive item. If he wishes to remember you at holiday time, accept with thanks and don't worry about returning the gesture.

The only time a secretary exchanges presents with her employer is after she has worked with him for a number of years. Of course, in this situation, you would exercise a certain amount of discretion and refrain from gifts of a personal nature.

GETTING ALONG WITH YOUR CO-WORKERS. A good portion of your daily life will be spent with the people around you in the office. Naturally, you will want your association to be as pleasant as possible. The biggest gripe the veterans have against the beginner is that the new girl often doesn't realize that privilege comes with responsibility. Miss Elizabeth Farrell, a supervisor of secretarial jobs in the New York investment counseling firm of Lionel D. Edie & Company, gives the following advice to beginners:

"Don't assume the privileges of your boss. If he is a V.P., he's the titled man—not you. Further, if you are a new young secretary, don't assume the privileges of older women."

You want to get started on the right foot with your co-workers; therefore you will not assume privileges until you are told you have earned them.

BE CAREFUL OF CLIQUES. In every office you are bound to find one or two closely knit groups better known as cliques. Whenever their jobs permit it, they seek out each other's company. Once in a while they will accept a new member into their confidence. What do you do if you happen to be the "lucky" one?

It isn't a good idea to join a group of this nature. Being part of a clique will naturally inhibit your relations with the rest of your co-workers, and may be frowned on by the management. For this reason you should stay clear of all private office societies, which have a habit of breeding dissent and jealousies with those who are not "in." Your reputation may gain, if anything, when it is known you were offered membership but turned it down.

► **Hint.** Don't try to gain friendships by becoming too intimate too quickly with people in the office. This is one time when familiarity may breed contempt, if you are not careful. Remember, many people prefer to keep their office associations apart from their private lives. Go slowly; you will have plenty of time later on to build lasting relationships.

EXPECT PEOPLE TO BE ONLY HUMAN. In every office you will have some people whom you look up to and others whom you dislike. This is human nature. If everyone had exactly the same temperament, it would be a dull world indeed.

Everyone has good and bad points; the idea is to accept both. For example, one girl may be really likeable, except for those "moody" days when she is short with her fellow workers. If you will remember that you probably have a few personality traits that your co-workers aren't too happy about, you should be able to take the moods of your co-workers in your stride.

► **Warning.** Don't try to be the office reformer. You may think that Sally is ruining her chances of becoming a successful secretary with her temper outbursts, but you're not the one to correct her, especially if you're a newcomer to the office.

GETTING ALONG WITH DIFFICULT CO-WORKERS. Suppose you have just been assigned to work with another secretary on a special project, and your friends hasten to tell you that the other girl is extremely difficult to get along with. Are you tempted to go in with a chip on your shoulder expecting the worst? Or will you undertake the job pleasantly with a spirit of cooperation?

Naturally you choose the latter course and try to be polite and helpful. Generally you will discover that gossip exaggerates and the other secretary is really quite nice. She may be only shy, and not good at making small talk.

On the other hand, if you know from your own experience that a co-worker delights in making life miserable for those around her, you are justified in taking preventive measures. Try to avoid the trouble-maker as much as possible. Should her behavior constitute serious offenses against company regulations, you may call them to the attention of a superior without feeling like a tattle-tale. However, be absolutely sure your conflict doesn't stem from a personality clash; even if you dislike her, she may be a good worker.

DEALING WITH THOSE BELOW YOU ON THE LADDER. A real secretary is more than a glorified typist; she has a position of responsibility, and she enjoys a certain status in the company ranks. Do you make the mistake of letting this go to your head, so that you find yourself being less courteous to people like mail boys, maintenance men, and others you may feel are below you on the ladder?

Good manners have nothing to do with title or position; you should extend them to everyone, just as you expect everyone to honor them. And perhaps you are forgetting that without these people your company could not function efficiently. If you haven't already discovered it, there are times when a stock clerk or a trainee in the duplicating department can be the person whose help you need most.

YOU HAVE TO GO THROUGH CHANNELS ON THE WAY DOWN, TOO. The principle of respecting rank within the company works on the way down, as well as on the way up. Suppose your employer has given you permission to pass some of your work on an important assignment to the typing pool. You know that one girl there does especially good work. Don't give the job directly to her. Instead, give it to her supervisor, and ask if she can assign the girl to it. It's another example of the Golden Rule. If you had an assistant (and you may well have) you wouldn't want anyone to give her work without first consulting you.

COURTESY IS IMPORTANT WITH SUBORDINATES. You may have the authority to put work on someone else's desk and just say "Have this done by three o'clock," but we hope you never would. The courteous secretary explains assignments and the necessity of having one completed quickly, and she never forgets to say "please." Once a girl understands that the job she is doing is important and that you are counting on her, she tries her best to please. The girl who has a rush job dumped in her lap with just a few curt instructions is not likely to care too much how she completes the assignment.

Courteous behavior will always make you a standout with everyone in the office, from the doorman to the president. A lady always has a smile and a cheerful greeting and she never forgets to say "thank you" for even a small courtesy.

BEWARE OF A "SUPERIOR" ATTITUDE. Some secretaries are courteous in a way that suggests they are bestowing a great favor. You should take care not to talk down to anyone in your office. They will only resent it, just as you would if you were in their position.

OFFICE ROMANCES. The office is a place of business, not a playground for romance and matrimony. One of the surest ways to jeopardize your position as a trusted secretary is to allow what should be your own private affairs to become a source of office gossip and kidding.

The office romance is always a potential bombshell. For example, what happens if someone discovers your alliance and chooses to make it the subject of malicious gossip? What happens if relations should cool, or, even worse, if you should sever your relationship with a quarrel, each trying not to show it to fellow workers?

The potential danger is even greater if you should become romantically involved with an executive in your company. Any indiscreet behavior on your part (or his) could adversely affect his career; it could cost you your job.

Your boss would never presume to interfere with your private life, but your office life is his business, and when it becomes a problem for him he is justified in doing something about it. The lesson is a simple one: be romantic, if you like, but be discreet!

OFFICE PARTIES. Traditionally, the office party is the time when everyone lets his or her hair down, only to regret it the next day. Even if parties in your office are infrequent, there is enough truth in this tradition to serve as a warning for the girl who would be a truly competent secretary.

A man wants his secretary to represent him well; he wants to be proud of the way she handles herself, whatever the occasion. Show your executive that you don't lose your head at office parties, and he will know that you can be counted on at business dinners and other functions to which you might accompany him.

HOW TO MAKE INTRODUCTIONS

At one time or another you will be called upon to perform introductions in your office. If you ever find this confusing, the following examples of how it's done should be helpful.

1. ***Introducing a male colleague to a woman employee.*** Present the man to the woman: "Miss Jones, may I introduce Mr. Allen?" Most business introductions are even briefer: "Miss Jones, this is Mr. Allen."

2. ***Introducing a man to two women.*** Simply say: "Miss Jones and Mrs. Brown: (this is) Mr. Arthur." If the situation were reversed and you were introducing two men to a woman, you would say, "Mrs. Allen, may I introduce Mr. Smith and Mr. White?", or "Mrs. Allen: (this is) Mr. Smith and Mr. White."

3. ***Introducing a distinguished person to your employer.*** If a third party is not available to perform the introduction you may say, "Judge Jenkins, may I present Mr. Bradley?" You may also say "Judge Jenkins, may I introduce Mr. Bradley?" The first form is more formal than the second.

4. ***Two men of equal age and status.*** Should you be introducing two men of equal age and status you needn't worry about which one you should mention first. A simple "Mr. Jones: Mr. Smith," will do.

The above illustrated situations are the ones you are most likely to encounter in the office. In addition here are three simple rules that will serve as the basis for any introductions you may be called upon to make. They are:

1. Introduce a man to a woman.
   "Miss Norton, this is Mr. Elliot."
2. Introduce a younger person to an older one.
   "Mr. Elder, may I introduce Mr. Smith?"
3. Introduce lower ranks to higher ranks.
   "Judge Hanson, may I introduce Mr. Elton?"

HOW TO ESCORT VISITORS TO SEE YOUR EMPLOYER. When a visitor arrives, check to be sure your employer is ready for the interview. Then you might say, "Please come with me, Mr. Client. Mr. Hansen will see you now." If the visitor is a woman, open the door to your employer's office and stand aside while she enters. If the visitor is a man, take your cue from him. Most men will go right on in when you open the door. Some, however, will hang back and wait for you to precede them into the office. When you see this is the case, make sure the visitor has a firm hold on the door, if it's the type that doesn't stay opened, and continue into the office. Then you can make the introduction.

When does a lady shake hands? If a man offers his hand, you should take it without hesitation. If a man does not offer you his hand, you may offer yours to him or not, as you choose. Either course is correct.

There are at least two exceptions:

- *High ranking (state) officials.* It is always up to them to make the first move toward shaking hands.

- *Foreign countries.* In some parts of the world, especially South America, shaking hands is a must. When you are abroad it is a good idea to offer your hand, since you'll never be considered rude for shaking hands, but you may commit a faux pas if you fail to do so.

3. HOW TO USE THE TELEPHONE CORRECTLY

Is your office telephone a liability, instead of an asset? The answer depends on whether you have learned to use the phone effectively. At home you may be able to get away with picking up the telephone on the fourth or fifth ring and using a simple "Hello" as greeting.. In a business office this is considered time consuming and discourteous. Use this chapter as your guide to greater telephone efficiency.

WHOSE RESPONSIBILITY IS IT? As secretary to a busy executive, a good portion of your working day will be taken up with placing and receiving telephone calls. These calls bring your employer a lot of information and a lot of headaches. Your job is to filter through the information and keep out the headaches, and through it all you must remain pleasant and polite. Study the following suggestions carefully and you will be prepared to do your best for your employer and your company every time you pick up the receiver.

THE IMPORTANCE OF A PLEASING VOICE. A salesman is often told that he *is* his company to those on whom he calls. In much the same way, your telephone voice may be the image of your company to people who deal with you over the phone.

Few of us are born with voices like angels, but we can all improve the voice and speech habits we have. Start now to develop a pleasing voice, paying special attention to the factors below.

Volume control. With some beginners the exuberance of youth hasn't worn off yet, and they tend to bellow cheerfully into the telephone. Just as bad is the shy young thing who can hardly be heard at the other end. Practice every day and work toward that middle ground, neither too loud nor too soft.

Give meaning to your voice. Study the tone of your voice. Be sure you are giving emphasis to your words and not speaking in a dull monotone. This gives a personal touch to your voice, makes a caller feel like he is talking to an interested person, not a robot.

Obey the speed limits. The average speaking rate for most people is 126 words per minute. Test yourself and see how close you come to this mark. Take a prepared speech, count the number of words in it, and read aloud for five minutes. Then take the total number of words spoken and divide by five for your average. If you are far off the mark in either direction, it is difficult to understand you over the telephone. Naturally, you aren't expected to speak exactly 126 words every minute either.

Speak clearly and distinctly. A most important factor is pronunciation. Businessmen don't want to waste time on the telephone asking you to repeat messages. Learn to speak distinctly, pronouncing every syllable. If you're in the habit of slurring words or skipping over syllables, then you need practice in pronunciation. Get a list of tongue twisters, the "Peter Piper picked a peck of pickled peppers" kind, and work on them until you are no longer requested to repeat information.

Get that friendly quality into your voice. Last but not least, you should have a friendly voice. Make the caller feel you are interested in him and what he has to say. Don't overdo it but try to perfect a blend of polit friendliness and office efficiency.

► **Hint.** Try to get hold of a tape recorder for your practice sessions. If you have never heard yourself speak before, you may be quite surprised. Few people recognize their voices the first time they hear them on a recorder. This is one of the best ways to discover your speech faults and to start correcting them.

WHY YOU SHOULD ANSWER PROMPTLY. In a business office the telephone should be answered on the first ring, certainly not later than the second. A busy executive becomes very annoyed when he has to sit out three, four or even five rings before someone picks up the receiver. Besides, this raises the question as to where you are, if not at your desk. Beginners sometimes forget the importance of the telephone. A vital call can come in at any moment. If you plan to be away from your desk for any length of time, arrange to have someone else answer your phone and take messages. If you are delayed in answering the phone, be sure to apologize to the caller for keeping him waiting.

You may be taking one call when a second comes in on another line. Wait for a break in the conversation and announce that you have another call and ask to be excused for a moment. Wait until the first caller gives you his okay before pushing the "Hold" button which cuts him off from the immediate line of conversation but keeps him connected to the office. Then take the second call. Apologize to your second caller for keeping him waiting and explain that you have a call on your other line and ask him if he will wait for a few minutes. If your first caller is going to engage the line for any length of time, be sure to notify the man on the second line so he can take the option of calling back at a more convenient time.

► **Warning.** When your employer has a caller on one line and a second call comes in on the other line, be sure you answer the correct line. Your employer will not take kindly to your interrupting his conversation with a buoyant "Good Afternoon, Smith & Company."

WHAT TO SAY WHEN YOU ANSWER THE TELEPHONE. When you answer your telephone you identify your company and then your office, "Martin Jones Company, Mr. Henry's office." If calls come through an office switchboard, it is not necessary to identify the company. Simply say "Mr. Henry's office, Miss Willis speaking," or just "Mr. Henry's office. Never answer a business phone with a plain "Hello." The caller only has to waste his time and yours by finding out if he has the right party.

HOW TO SCREEN TELEPHONE CALLS. One of your more important jobs as a secretary will involve the screening of telephone calls, in order that your employer is not bothered by cranks and others seeking to waste his valuable time. Your methods of evasion will vary according to the nature of the intruder. Here are two typical examples:

The mystery man. The mystery man must always talk to your employer at once and will tell you it's "a matter of vital importance" in an effort to be connected without any questions. Don't be thrown into a panic. Remember that a man with a genuine emergency will state his name and business in short order. Most businessmen don't want their secretaries to put unidentified callers on the line, and therefore will have no objections to giving this information to colleagues' secretaries. If a man won't tell you his name or the reason for his call, you must simply refuse to connect him.

The cranks and troublemakers. Members of this group are most trying. When they find out they are not going to be connected, they sometimes become belligerent and provoking. Above all, don't lose your temper and start an argument. Here is a typical example of how one secretary handled a troublemaker:

"Mr. Hansen's office, Miss Carney speaking."
"I want to talk to Mr. Hansen."
"May I have your name, sir?"
"I'm Tom Smith."
"May I tell Mr. Hansen the reason for your call, Mr. Smith?"
"He fired my cousin yesterday, and I intend to talk to him about it."
"I'm sorry, but Mr. Hansen is very busy right now. Perhaps you would like to write him a letter about the situation. If you will mark it 'Personal', I will see that it comes to his attention."
"No, I demand to talk to him."
"I'm very sorry, Mr. Smith, but I can't help you. Good-bye."

This is one situation where you are justified in hanging up before the other party has quite finished speaking. To prolong such a conversation would only strain matters further, and force you into an argumentative position. When it is obvious that your caller is not going to take the hint, just apologize and hang up. But don't be brusque: keep your voice even and calm.

HOW TO TRANSFER A CALL. If you are switching your caller off to the "Hold" line or to a second line that is open while you signal the operator, be sure to explain to him what is about to happen or he might think he is being cut off. Then flash for the operator by depressing the receiver buttons slowly. Between depressions, listen for the operator. When she answers, say "Please transfer this call to extension 577." She will take over from there.

When your telephone doesn't have a hold button or a second line free, it will be necessary for you to keep your caller on the open line while you speak to the operator. When the operator answers, don't say "This guy wants production;" beginners sometimes do this, forgetting that in an open line situation the caller can hear every word spoken to the switchboard operator.

HOW TO HANDLE VICTIMS OF THE RUN-AROUND. Once in a while you get an unfortunate caller who has been transferred to seven different offices, and still hasn't found the man he is seeking. By this time he is likely to be audibly annoyed, especially when asked again who he is looking for. When you encounter such a caller and you aren't sure just whom he should talk to, tell him so and offer to call him back when you have the information. You can make a friend or an enemy for the company in a situation of this nature, depending on your behavior.

► **Hint.** Take the caller's name and telephone number and arrange to have his party call him. This will make him infinitely happier than if you transfer him again, even if it is to the right party.

Of course, you should never start someone on a wild goose chase. Whenever you have any doubt about where a call belongs, get the caller's name and number and then go after the correct information. Your caller would much rather wait a little while and receive one telephone call than have to repeat his story six or seven times as he gets bounced through the company.

HOW TO PLACE LONG DISTANCE AND SPECIAL CALLS. A prime consideration in making long distance calls is the cost. Long distance calls fall into several categories and the charges vary according to the type and length of the call. These calls are usually made through the operator, unless it is a station-to-station call, in which case you may be able to use direct dialing with the new area code system.

Person-To-Person Call. This is a call between individuals. The charges do not begin until the specified parties are on the line. Should you be calling Mr. Allen at Forbes Enterprises, your charges would not start until your employer and Mr. Allen actually began their conversation. If Mr. Allen's secretary had answered the phone, the operator would have conversed with her and you would not be connected until Mr. Allen himself was on the line. On a person-to-person call you may not talk with anyone but the party to whom you are addressing the call. If that party is not available, there is no charge.

Station-To-Station Call. A station-to-station call is billed at a cheaper rate than a person-to-person call, but charges start as soon as someone at the other end picks up the phone. Therefore, you must be sure that the person you are trying to contact will be available.

Appointment Call. Perhaps your employer wants a person-to-person call placed at a certain hour. All you have to do is tell the outside operator whom you wish to contact and the time you want the call to be put through. At the appointed hour the operator will contact you and ask if you are ready to have the call placed. Then, while you remain on the wire, she will make the connection. There is no extra charge for this service. The regular person-to-person rates apply.

Messenger Call. Your employer can even place a call to a person who does not have a telephone. You must notify the operator at the point you are calling and have her send out an authorized messenger to find your party. A charge for the messenger service is assessed, even if your party cannot be located. You will not be charged for the call, however, unless your party is put on the line.

Conference Call. Your employer can converse with two or more people in different cities simultaneously. No special equipment is needed; simply ask for the conference operator and give her the names of those you want connected.

Overseas Call. Transoceanic cables now make it possible for you to call practically any city in the world. The charge for such a call naturally will be higher than for a call within the United States. Simply notify your operator that you wish to make an overseas call and then tell her the name of the country you are calling.

► **Warning.** Be sure to check your time zones before calling. Two o'clock in the afternoon at your office might be two o'clock in the morning at your destination.

Calls to Ships, Trains, Automobiles. Many mobile units now carry radio telephones. When you want to place a call to a mobile unit, just ask your operator for the mobile service operator or the marine operator. These special operators will handle your calls.

HOW ARE LONG DISTANCE CHARGES COMPUTED? There is a flat charge for the first three minutes of a long distance call. After that you are charged, at another rate, for each additional minute of conversation. The rates on a call depend on the distance between the calling points, the kind of call you are making and the time of day when the call is made.

Special reduced rates are in effect every evening between 6:00 P.M. and 4:30 A.M. and all day Sunday. You can effect a considerable saving if you can arrange calls during these periods.

When making a long distance call, you may make it collect. The person being called is notified of the charge in advance and should he refuse it, the call is simply canceled. There is no extra charge for a collect call.

You may make a long distance call from another phone and charge it to your number. However, the operator will contact your number to be sure the charges will be accepted before she makes the connection, so be certain you have someone at your phone to authorize the call.

POINTS TO REMEMBER WHEN MAKING A LONG DISTANCE CALL.

Now you may dial direct any place in the United States, including Alaska, Hawaii, and Puerto Rico, by use of an area code. Here is how it works. Suppose you are in New York City and wish to call NO 5-7474 in Portland, Oregon. The area code for Oregon is 503. Simply dial 503, then dial NO 5-7474. There is a complete list of area codes in your telephone directory. Most directories also include a list of rates between important cities which you can use as a basis for estimating the cost of your calls.

On some occasions you may find it necessary to work with the operator. When this happens you should give her the following information, in order:

1. The city where your party is located
2. The telephone number of your party, including the area code
3. The name of the person you are calling, if it is a person-to-person call
4. Your own number

Remain on the line so you can answer any further questions from the operator. For example, if your party is not available you will have to either name a substitute or cancel the call. When the connection is made, say "Mr. Smith is waiting. Please hold the line." In this fashion charges will not begin until your employer is on the line.

Remember, costs mount by the minute. Have all your information ready before you pick up the receiver, and see that your employer has what he will need. You don't want to waste anyone's time, or money, at either end, so be prepared.

HOW TO RECEIVE A LONG DISTANCE CALL. Whenever you receive a long distance call, handle it as quickly and as efficiently as possible. If you have to turn the call over to your employer or someone else in the office, try to make the connection without delay. Even when you have a person-to-person call, where the charges won't start until both parties are on the line, it is poor etiquette to keep anyone waiting on the telephone. If it's a station-to-station call, every minute is costing your caller money.

Occasionally a long distance call will come for your employer when he is not in the office. If the caller cannot speak with anyone else, you will have to take the name and number of the caller from the operator and have your employer call back. The operator will give you the name of the city calling and her own operator's number. You will need all of this information to return the call.

for instance: The operator may tell you "This is operator 787 in Los Angeles. Your caller is Mr. Nathan, Drury 5-9000." When you are ready to return the call, contact the operator in your city and say "May I have operator 787 in Los Angeles." Once you have operator 787 you say "I am returning a call from Mr. Nathan, Drury 5-9000." The operator will take over and handle the connection between your employer and Mr. Nathan.

When a collect call comes in, your employer will tell you whether or not to accept it. Some companies accept all collect calls while others will only take them from employees or salesmen. Sometimes a collect call is expected from a client in which case you will have instructions in advance to accept the charges.

If you have any doubts about taking a collect call, ask the operator to wait while you check with your employer, or have the call transferred to him and let him make the decision.

HOW TO EXERCISE DISCRETION ON THE TELEPHONE. The best way to guard confidential information on the telephone is to follow one simple axiom—THINK BEFORE YOU SPEAK. If an unknown caller requests confidential information, you refuse him, naturally. But what do you do when the caller is one of your employer's co-workers, or perhaps even one of his superiors? Your best bet is to refer the call to your employer. Simply say "Mr. Jones has that information. I'll put you through to him." If you are known to have the information, you may say that your employer happens to have it at the moment and let him take it from there.

If you should find it necessary to interrupt a call to answer a question or greet someone who has come into the office, wait for a break in the conversation and say "Can you excuse me for a minute, please? Someone has just come into the office." Then you may either put your hand over the mouthpiece or switch your caller to the "Hold" line. If you choose the latter method, be sure to inform your caller about what you are doing so he will know he is not being cut off.

Occasionally you may have to leave a live receiver on your desk while you look up information in your files for the caller. Don't engage in any unnecessary conversation while you are performing this task, and don't let a friend who happens to come into the office start chatting either. Point to the receiver and motion to the person to keep her voice down. Stray remarks, or perhaps laughter, overheard by callers can be easily misinterpreted.

PERSONAL CALLS AT THE OFFICE. If you have the privilege of making personal calls at the office, don't abuse it. One department head had this to say about personal calls:

"Keep them at a minimum and make them extremely brief. Don't permit people to call you just to chat. If you must make a call, make it when your desk is not busy and by no means keep talking when someone else is standing at your desk waiting for attention. If you are buzzed by the man for whom you work, excuse yourself immediately and cut the call off."

► **Remember.** Receiving and making personal calls is a privilege, not a right. Constant abuse will only force your employer to withdraw the practice entirely. Your work must come above everything else while you are in the office.

4. HOW TO AVOID GRAMMATICAL MISTAKES IN YOUR CORRESPONDENCE

Letters, the lifeline of business communication, carry the image of your company wherever they go. That image will be poor unless the grammar and punctuation in those letters is good, and, like it or not, this is your responsibility, just as neatness is. Any businessman who receives a letter containing errors in grammar develops a poor impression of the writer and his organization.

If your executive sometimes is too rushed to be careful in his dictating, he counts on you to be extra careful in your transcription. This doesn't mean that you point out every error to your employer; it is part of your job to make obvious corrections without comment.

Let's discuss some of the problems you will come across.

COMMON ERRORS IN GRAMMAR

Here are five areas where errors are most likely to occur. Keep your eyes open for them.

AGREEMENT OF SUBJECT AND VERB. The subject and verb of a sentence must always agree in person and number. Most errors occur when words intervene between the subject and the verb. These rules should help you keep agreement.

(a) *When you have a compound subject.* A plural verb is used when two or more subjects are in the third person and are joined by *and*. The exception to this rule is when both nouns refer to the same person or thing.

for instance: The president and vice-president *are* in conference. The vice-president and general manager *is* in Chicago.

(b) *When you have alternative subjects.* When alternative subjects differ in person and number, the verb takes its number from the part of the subject nearest the verb.

for instance: Neither Miss Adams nor the girls in the steno pool *were* notified of the change.

(c) *When there is a noun between the subject and verb.* The verb must agree with the subject, regardless of the noun between.

for instance: Mr. Smith, with Mr. Baker and Miss Lane, *is* in the president's office.

(d) *When you have a subordinate clause.* In a subordinate clause, the subject of the *clause,* not the main subject of the sentence, gives the verb its number.

for instance: His coat is one of [those that *are* hanging on the second rack].

(e) *When the subject follows the verb.* Once again, the verb must agree in number with the subject, regardless of position.

for instance: Under the desk *are* the controls.

(f) *When the subject and predicate nominative differ in number.* A predicate nominative always amplifies the thought presented in the ubject, even though it completes the verb. However, should the subect and predicate nominative disagree in number, the verb must agree vith the subject.

for instance: Night classes *are* [the answer for the slow learner].

The answer for the slow learner is the predicate nominative and is ingular, but the subject of the sentence (classes) is plural, therefore, he plural verb "are."

(g) *When you have collective nouns.* A collective noun is usually considered to be singular in number; therefore, the verb is also singular. The only time a collective noun may be regarded as plural is when the sentence makes it clear that the subject refers to members of a group and not the group as a whole.

for instance: The minority *is* demanding its share of speaking time. The minority *are* arguing about their share of speaking time.

(h) *When you have subjects plural in form but singular in meaning.* Subjects such as *politics* or *mathematics* take singular verbs when used strictly as a name. When you denote qualities, however, you use a plural verb.

for instance: Mathematics *is* an interesting subject.
After the review, we discovered that his mathematics *were* wrong.

SEQUENCE OF TENSES. When you have two or more verbs in a sentence the tense indicates the time relationship. A change in tense denotes a change in time. Here are some examples of how to use different tenses properly.

(a) When stating a universal truth, you will generally use the present tense, even though the main verb is in the past tense.

for instance: Years ago he learned that knowledge *is* never wasted.

(b) When you are writing in the past tense and want to mention a preceding event, you should employ the past perfect tense.

for instance: He checked the report that he *had written* last month.

(c) When you employ the future tense in a main clause, use the present tense in a dependent clause.

for instance: The order will be accepted as soon as the account *is* checked.

(d) Be sure to use the perfect participle (not the present participle) when you want to denote an action that has been completed at the time indicated by the main verb.

for instance: She will return the books to the library, *having finished* her research work.

THE SUBJUNCTIVE. When you wish to express a conditional or desirable idea, or the like, you use the subjunctive mood of the verb.

(a) When stating a condition contrary to fact, you should use the subjunctive. These statements are usually prefaced by *if* or *wish.*

for instance: If you were a little more experienced, I would give you the job.

(b) When a clause is introduced by *that* and the main verb denotes necessity, demand or recommendation, you should use the subjunctive.

for instance: He suggested that she *finish* [not *finishes*] the work.

(c) To express a motion, resolution or ruling in formal writing, use the subjunctive.

for instance: The finance committee ruled that the members finance the innovations on the club house.

(d) When you want to denote a supposition or condition in clauses introduced by *as if* or *as though,* use the past subjunctive.

for instance: It appears as though a report *were* [not *is*] missing.

PRONOUNS. Whenever you use a pronoun, you are replacing a noun. Therefore, you must be sure the pronoun agrees in person, number and gender with the noun it is replacing. Here are some principles to follow:

(a) *When pronouns are referring to collective nouns.* The number (singular or plural) of the noun determines the number of the pronoun.

For instance: The committee extended its influence to get the bill accepted. (In this case the committee is acting as one, therefore, the pronoun [its] is singular.) The committee have been arguing as to their influence in the club. (Here we refer to the committee as a group of individuals, hence the plural pronoun [their].)

(b) *When you have alternative subjects.* When both subjects are obviously singular, you use a singular pronoun.

for instance: Neither John nor Henry reached *his* goal.

The part of the subject nearest the pronoun determines the number of the pronoun when you have alternative subjects.

for instance: Neither John nor his colleagues reached *their* goal.

(c) *An indefinite pronoun* is always singular and always employs a singular verb and singular pronouns.

for instance: Everyone was trying to reach *his* goal.

AMBIGUOUS MODIFIERS. You can easily confuse your reader when you place a modifier between two nouns and fail to clarify with which noun the modifier belongs.

for instance: Men who smoke constantly have bad coughs. (What does *constantly* modify?) To make the meaning clear for the reader you would have to say: Men who constantly smoke have bad coughs.

Watch out for ambiguous references to pronouns. Make sure the reference between your noun and pronoun is clear.

for instance: Mr. Jones made Henry a supervisor even though he had only been with the company for seven months. (Who had been with the firm seven months—Mr. Jones or Henry?) A better way to phrase this would be: Mr. Jones, although he had been with the company only seven months, made Henry a supervisor.

CONSISTENCY IN SENTENCE STRUCTURE. Similar word structures are necessary in a sentence where two or more ideas are used in the same way. Coordinating connectives (but, for, nor, or, and) are generally used to connect the ideas. Here are some areas to watch out for:

(a) *Compounds.* The same parts of speech must be used when you have words in a parallel structure.

for instance: (Wrong) A man must be brave and have intelligence to explore outer space.

(Correct) A man must be brave and intelligent to explore outer space.

(b) *Inconsistency in a series.* Inconsistent forms occasionally appear late in a series when more than two items occupy parallel position.

for instance: (Wrong) He is bright, handsome, witty and all the attributes of a likeable person.

(Correct) He is bright, handsome, witty and likeable.

(c) *Faulty comparisons.* When you make comparisons you must use parallel forms and word order. Parallel positions must represent comparable ideas if your sentence is to be easily understood.

for instance: (Wrong) The specialist felt his job required more knowledge than a general practitioner.

(Correct) The specialist felt his job required more knowledge than the job of a general practitioner.

(d) *False parallelism.* Beware of putting into parallel form expressions that do not parallel one another.

for instance: This is the correct form:

The mechanics are in the shop working on the cars. (*not* The mechanics are in the shop and working on the cars.)

COMMON MISTAKES IN PUNCTUATION

Even though you have studied punctuation in grammar school, high school, and possibly business school or college, you can probably use some brushing up. Here are the rules concerning the most common punctuation marks.

USE OF THE COMMA. Perhaps the most misunderstood of all punctuation marks is the comma. Beginning secretaries tend to drop commas here and there down the page when they think a sentence is too long. Or they forget the comma completely and let sentences run on unchecked. The comma is a warning to the reader, a rest or pause between two ideas. Mistakes in punctuation can result in serious misunderstandings. At the very least they will give a bad impression of your employer's standards.

Unfortunately, rules for the use of the comma aren't hard and fast. You've probably heard the terms *open punctuation* and *close punctuation,* used mostly in reference to commas. Open punctuation means using commas only where they are absolutely necessary for clarity.

Close punctuation means that you use commas wherever the grammatical construction permits. For business use you will generally follow the theory of open punctuation. This will keep your letters neat and readable.

Example of Close Punctuation—A gun, which, under certain circumstances, causes death, can be rendered totally harmless by removing the firing pin.

Example of Open Punctuation—A gun, which under certain circumstances causes death, can be rendered totally harmless by removing the firing pin.

Now let's have a review of proper usage.

(a) *Use of the comma with conjunctions.* Commas are always placed before true co-ordinating conjunctions (yet, nor, neither, for, or, but, and) when they separate two independent clauses in a compound sentence.

for instance: Joe is smart and quick, but he needs more experience. Jeff is a good newspaperman, and he has been given the editor's job on a month's trial basis.

If clauses are short and strongly related, you may omit the comma before *and*.

for instance: The excavation was completed today and the foundation will be poured tomorrow.

► **Warning.** *Therefore, however, accordingly,* and *consequently* are not true co-ordinating conjunctions. Use a semi-colon before these words, not a comma.

(b) *Setting off unnecessary elements.* A word, phrase or clause that is not absolutely essential to a sentence may be set off in commas; this is non restrictive material. Restrictive material is that which is essential to the meaning of the sentence. You would never set off restrictive material in commas.

for instance: Miss Adams, the stenographic supervisor [non-restrictive], retired after thirty years with the firm.

(c) *The comma with a series.* When you have a series of words, phrases or clauses, you should set them off with commas.

for instance: The book covered grammar, spelling, and punctuation. (Remember to retain the comma between the last two items in the series, even if *and* is used. This prevents any possible misunderstanding of your meaning.)

You never place a comma after the last item in a series except when the verb follows the last item and there is no intervening conjunction.

for instance: Telephone, typewriter, dictating machine, photo machine, are all used by the modern secretary.

When you have a sentence with three or more parts, the clauses form a series and are punctuated with commas.

for instance: The boss shouted, the secretary turned red, and the clerks waited for the storm to break.

(d) *Between adjectives.* When a series of adjectives have the same value and refer to the same noun, they should be separated with commas. Do not use commas when adjectives are not of equal value.

for instance: She is a bright, young, attractive girl. The new white modern building houses the investment company. (*Bright, young,* and *attractive* are adjectives of equal value while *new white modern* are not.)

(e) *The comma with introductory and parenthetic elements.* You should place commas after introductory words, phrases and clauses, although the usage may vary on occasion. Commas are almost always placed after long introductory elements and those containing verb forms.

for instance: After the storm subsided, there was a beautiful rainbow.

Parenthetical and defining words and phrases are set off in commas unless they have a close and smooth connection with the rest of the sentence.

for instance: He can, I believe, meet the requirements. She *was definitely the prettiest* girl in the room. (Definitely reads smoothly without being set off.)

(f) *Use of the comma to denote omission.* When you want to indicate the absence of an obvious word, you may use a comma.

for instance: Joan completed the first book; Jane, the second. (Comma replaces *completed.*)

(g) *Using the comma with quotations.* There are three uses for the comma when you are quoting:

(1) to set off the phrase that identifies the speaker

(2) before a short quotation when it is introduced by an explanatory phrase

(3) between the quotation and identifying phrase.

for instance: Sally moaned, "I'll never finish this job by five o'clock."

"I'll never," Sally moaned, "finish this job by five o'clock."

"I'll never finish this job by five o'clock," moaned Sally.

► **Remember.** The comma is always placed *inside* the quotation marks.

(h) *Using the comma with dates and addresses.* The day of the month is always separated from the year by a comma. The month is separated from the year by a comma when no day is given. A city is always separated from a state by a comma. It is optional whether you place a comma after a state to separate it from the rest of the sentence.

for instance: The report is due April 1, 1964.
The report is due in April, 1964.
The Adams Company in Chelsey, California are opening a new office in Los Angeles.

(i) *Using the comma with numbers.* When you write a figure in the thousands, you should use a comma, unless the numbers refer to a house address, room, post office box, or telephone number.

for instance: $19,408.27 2323 Chestnut Street

(j) *Using the comma with titles.* A comma is always placed between a name and *Sr., Inc., Ltd.,* and so on. If there is an *of* indicating place or position, no comma is used.

for instance: James Johnson, Sr. Mr. Carter of Jones Company

HOW TO USE QUOTATION MARKS. You use quotation marks only when you are using another person's exact words. Do not use quotation marks if the name of the speaker is set off by a colon from the quoted material.

for instance: Jane asked, "Do you have a book on casserole cooking?" Jane went to the library and asked for "a book on casserole cooking."

or

Librarian: May I help you,
Jane: I would like a book on casserole cooking.

When you have brief phrases uttered by more than one person, you must enclose each phrase in quotation marks. The entire group of phrases may be enclosed in one set of quotation marks when only one speaker is involved.

for instance: The announcement concerning the new filing procedure evoked several comments. "Whose idea was that?" "It will never work." "Nobody will be able to find anything!" were a few of the offerings.
When informed of the new filing procedure, Sally said "Whose idea was that? It will never work. Nobody will be able to find anything."

(a) *How to use quotation marks with long quotations.* Sometimes quoted material will be more than one paragraph in length. When this happens, be sure to place quotation marks at the beginning of each paragraph but at the close of the last paragraph only. You may omit the quotation marks only if you indent all the paragraphs from both margins, and indicate in the text that the indented material is a quote.

(b) *How to use quotation marks with unique terms.* The first time you use an unusual word or phrase, enclose it in quotation marks. This also applies to words with special trade meanings. Also enclose a word or phrase in quotation marks when it is accompanied by its definition.

for instance: A "parry" in fencing is a defensive maneuver designed to halt an adversary's attack.

(c) *How to use quotation marks with titles.* Place quotation marks around the titles of articles, books, chapters or parts of books, operas, paintings, pamphlets, plays, motion pictures, poems, sketches and songs. Quotation marks should not be used with the names of periodicals; the Bible or the names of its books; movements of a symphony, concerto, or other compositions; or names of numbered compositions.

(d) *What to do with quotes within quotes.* Use single quotation marks to set off a quotation within a quotation. If you have still another quotation within that quotation, you can revert back to the double quotation marks.

for instance: Carol told her friends at lunch, "Mr. Ethan is really pleased about the way everyone pitched in last week. He said, 'Someone should give citations to you all for a job well done.' "

(e) *How to use quotation marks with other punctuation.* There are three general rules to follow:

(1) A period or comma is always placed within the quotation marks.

(2) Colons and semicolons are always placed outside the quotation marks.

(3) Question marks and exclamation points can come inside or outside the quotation marks, depending on whether the question mark or exclamation point is part of the actual quote.

for instance: She said, "I understand," but then failed to do the job correctly.

She asked, "Do you want this work completed by three o'clock?"

Didn't she say, "The file is in Mr. Allen's office"?

HOW TO USE THE COLON. The most common use of the colon for a secretary is after the salutation of a business letter.

for instance: Dear Sir: Dear Mr. Scott:

(a) *Using a colon to introduce lists.* Lists, series or tabulations may be introduced by a colon. When the colon is used as a replacement for "that is" or "for example," the terms themselves should not appear. A colon indicates that there is more material coming.

for instance: The following items may be ordered from the stock room: pencils, typewriter ribbons, carbon paper, letterhead paper, envelopes, paper clips, glue.

(b) *Other uses for the colon.* Here are three areas where you would use the colon:

(1) when indicating clock time (3:00 a.m.)

(2) when separating the verse and chapter in reference to the Bible (Mark 1:3)

(3) when separating the name of the city of publication from the name of the publisher when you have a reference to a publication in a footnote (Englewood Cliffs, New Jersey: Prentice-Hall, Inc.)

HOW TO USE THE SEMICOLON. The semicolon is similar in use to the comma, except that the semicolon indicates a more definite break in thought. You use a semicolon whenever you feel the comma does not emphasize the break strongly enough.

(a) *How to use the semicolon in a compound sentence.* When a comma and conjunction is eliminated, you may use a semicolon to separate parts of a compound sentence.

for instance: The cars are all lined up; the race can begin.

(b) *How to use a semicolon with long, involved clauses.* A semicolon is used to separate long, involved clauses, or clauses that are punctuated with commas within themselves.

(c) *How to use a semicolon with a series.* Unless the items in a series are short and simple, use semicolons to separate them. Semicolons may also be used to separate items that contain commas.

(d) *How to use a semicolon with conjunctive adverbs.* A semicolon is placed before an adverb when the adverb is acting as a conjunction. Adverbs that are used as conjunctions are *also, accordingly, besides, furthermore, however, hence, consequently, moreover, nevertheless, likewise, indeed, so, otherwise, similarly, thus, still* and *therefore.*

for instance: The report must be finished tonight; therefore you will have to work late.

(e) *Using a semicolon with other punctuation:* Semicolons are always placed outside of quotation marks.

If the construction of the sentence requires a semicolon, you place it after the closing parentheses. A semicolon or comma is never used before an expression enclosed in parentheses.

WHEN TO CAPITALIZE WORDS

Capitalization will vary according to circumstances. At one time you will capitalize a word, while in another situation you will use a small letter. Sometimes it is only a matter of choice, as either way would be correct. Where you have a choice, be consistent; once you choose to capitalize a word, you must capitalize it all the way through. You will find, though, that the present trend is toward less capitalization.

Here are the rules to follow:

(a) *Personal titles.* Capitalize all titles (business, religious, civil, titles of respect or honor) under these three circumstances:

(1) when you find them immediately before a name
(2) when you find them standing alone and referring to a specific person
(3) when you find them used in direct address as synonyms of proper names

You need not capitalize business, civil, or religious titles when they come after a name, except on the inside address of a business letter. Sometimes, however, companies make it a practice to capitalize titles out of courtesy.

(b) *Family titles.* When *Father, Mother, Aunt* and the like are used as titles or names, you capitalize them. You do not capitalize them when they merely refer to the persons.

for instance: Did you know that Aunt Alice will be in town next week? Your aunt and uncle will be in town next week.

(c) *Geographic terms.* Always capitalize geographic names. Words such as *river, street, ocean, east* and *north* are capitalized when they are part of a name, i.e. Hudson River, Chestnut Street, Pacific Ocean. If a locality has a popular or special descriptive name, you should capitalize it. *North, East, South, West* and their derivatives are capitalized only when they refer to sections of the country, not when they are used as simple directions.

(d) *Capitalization of van, von and de.* Van, von and de are capitalized when used in North American or English names. But you would not capitalize von, van and de when used in foreign names, unless the names begin the sentence or stand by themselves within the sentence. These are just general rules; however, the owner of the name has the final say about how it should appear.

(e) *Capitalization of official bodies.* The names of legislative, administrative, and deliberative bodies, domestic and foreign, are always capitalized. The word *legislature* is capitalized when it stands alone or refers to a particular body. You need not capitalize *legislature* when it is used with the name of a state, unless the precise designation is given. *State* and *Commonwealth* are capitalized when they are part of a name and when they stand alone, if they are applied to specific states or commonwealths.

(f) *Capitalization of governmental subdivisions.* You can always capitalize *federal* when it is part of a title. Either upper or lower case may be used when *federal* is employed as an adjective referring to a specific government. Federal is never capitalized when it is used as a general term.

The words *government* and *administration,* when used in reference to the government holding power in the country, are always capitalized. You would also capitalize government and administration when used as substitute titles for a political party in power.

When used as part of a name, you capitalize *department, ward, precinct, district, county, city* and *committee.* You do not capitalize these words when they stand alone or are used as general terms.

(g) *Capitalization of proper nouns.* Proper nouns and words used as proper nouns are always capitalized. Generally speaking, you would capitalize adjectives derived from proper nouns; however, words that have lost their association with proper nouns after long use are not capitalized.

(h) *Capitalization of religious terms.* The following should be capitalized:

- (1) all reference to the Deity or any member of the Christian Trinity or the Virgin Mary.
- (2) personal pronouns referring to the above, unless the pronoun closely follows the noun.
- (3) names of all religions, their heads, their followers and their sacred writings.
- (4) all names for books and divisions, versions and editions of the Bible.
- (5) religious denominations, monastic orders and their followers.
- (6) ecclesiastical terms and theological terms used with definite application.
- (7) title of a church dignitary when used with the name or when standing alone and applying to a specific person.

Do not capitalize:

- (1) relative pronouns such as *who, whom* and *whose.*
- (2) *god* and *goddess* when used in a general sense.
- (3) adjectives such as *scriptural* and *apocryphal.*
- (4) deacon, cantor, vicar, rector, rabbi, priest, minister, father or elder, unless they are used with the proper name or as a form of address.

(i) *Capitalization of trade names.* Copyrighted trade names must be capitalized. Years of use may reduce a trade name to a common noun but manufacturers still have the right to insist that you capitalize the names of their products.

(j) *Capitalization of heavenly bodies.* The words *moon, earth, stars,* and *sun* are not capitalized unless they are personified.

Examples: The moon was very bright last night.
All sailors learn how to use the North Star as a navigational guide.

All the names of stars, planets, and constellations—even their imaginative names—are capitalized.

Examples: Saturn, Polaris, Milky Way, Ursa Major, Big Dipper.

(k) *Capitalization of the first word of a sentence or line of poetry.* The first word in every sentence is always capitalized. One exception is when you have a complete sentence within parentheses within another sentence. With a poem, the first word of each line is capitalized, providing the poet isn't striving for a special effect, in which case you would follow his style. Capitalize the first word of a direct quotation, if the quotation is a complete sentence.

(l) *Capitalization of quoted material.* The first word of a quoted passage is capitalized, if the quoted material is an exact quotation and is a complete sentence. Lower case is used for quotations that do not make a complete sentence. Indirect quotations are not capitalized. The second part of a broken quotation is not capitalized unless it is a complete sentence.

(m) *Capitalization of headings and titles.* All important words in headings should be capitalized, including nouns, pronouns, adverbs, verbs and adjectives. Lower case is used for articles, conjunctions and prepositions. Prepositions of five or more letters may be capitalized if you wish.

To in the infinitive form may be capitalized, but lower case is preferable. Capitalize articles, prepositions and conjunctions that immediately follow a marked break indicated by a colon or dash in a title.

(n) *Capitalization of hyphenated words.* Hyphenated words are capitalized according to the way the parts would be written if they stood alone. In other words, if both parts are capitalized on their own, then both parts are capitalized in the hyphenated form.

(o) *Capitalization of references to numbered material.* References to numbered parts of compositions in typewritten work are capitalized. The lower case is preferable for the noun when "No." is placed between the noun and the numeral.

(p) *Capitalization of names of things personified.* The name of something personified is always capitalized for emphasis.

COMPOUND TERMS

Two or more words written separately but representing one idea make what is known as a compound term. There are no set rules concerning the forming of compounds; authorities differ and the language keeps changing. However, once you choose an acceptable form, use only that form; you should be consistent. Never switch from one form to another, especially in the same letter.

(a) *Compound adjectives.* These are words and phrases brought together to describe nouns. Two or more words used as an adjective before a noun are hyphenated. This includes color variations used as adjectives, i.e. blue-green, sky-blue, etc. If the words follow the noun, don't hyphenate.

Examples: two-car garage — the garage was the two car type
emerald-green sweater

When a compound adjective is formed by combining a present participle with a noun, adjective, or adverb, it should be hyphenated providing it precedes the noun it modifies. However, some of these compounds have become established members of the compound family and are always hyphenated whenever they appear, i.e. fur-bearing, far-reaching, etc.

(b) *What about adverbs?* A hyphen is never used to connect an adverb and an adjective. Also, never use a hyphen between an adverb ending in *ly* and a past participle.

Example: beautifully finished cabinet

(c) *Hyphenating nationalities.* Use a hyphen between two or more words when you want to show that the person or thing shares in the qualities of both.

Example: Irish-American

(d) *Hyphenating fractions.* When numerator and denominator are both one word forms, they may be hyphenated. Never use a hyphen between numerator and denominator if one of them already contains a hyphen, or the fraction is used as a noun.

Examples: sixty-nine hundredths — one third of our floor space
one-fourth interest

(e) *Hyphenating coined phrases.* You should always hyphenate a coined phrase or popularized saying of the times.

Examples: haul-it-yourself trailers
buy-now-pay-later

(f) *Hyphenating titles.* Titles are not hyphenated unless they are two nouns of equal value. In other words, the person mentioned takes part in the character of both nouns.

Example: Vice President-Treasurer

(g) *Hyphenating prefixes.* You do not use a hyphen with the following prefixes unless they are used with a proper noun: *inter-, non-, semi-, sub-*. However, you would use a hyphen with the prefix *self-*.

Examples: subnormal
self-appraisal

(h) *When you have plurals of compound terms.* In order to form the plural of a compound term, you make the most important word in the term plural. Find out which word denotes the principal title and you will have the most important word. With civilian titles the *s* is usually added to the first word, as this usually denotes the position held.

Generally, you will form the plural of military titles by adding *s* to the second word, which is normally the most important. An exception would be the plural of *sergeant major* which is formed on the first word since sergeant is the actual rank, not major.

Examples: major generals (*general* is the rank, not *major*)
heirs apparent (they are *heirs*, not *apparents*)
adjutants general (*adjutants* [assistants] is the main designation, not *general*)
notaries public (they are *notaries*, not *publics*)

RULES FOR USING THE HYPHEN

In addition to its use with compound terms, there are two more areas where you would employ a hyphen:

(a) *Hyphenated words in a series.* When you have a series of hyphenated words using a common base, the hyphen is placed after the first element of each word and the base is written after the last element only.

Examples: a five-, ten-, or fifteen-year economic plan
regular- and compact-size cars
long- and short-term notes

(b) *Indicating time spans.* A hyphen is used to indicate a span of time, except when the words *from* or *between* are used, in which case you would omit the hyphen.

Examples: between 1972 and 1975
during the years 1972-1982
from 1972 to 1974

IN CLOSING. These are your grammar rules. Keep them handy and refer to them often. In a little while they will become second nature to you and you will be well on your way to the top of your profession.

5. TIPS ON DICTATION AND TYPING

Some secretaries work harder, yet accomplish less, than they should. Do you make this mistake? You might, if you aren't putting into daily use the suggestions in this section, which deals with typing and dictation. These are the activities that account for the major portion of the average secretary's time—and offer the biggest opportunity for saving time and effort on the job.

HELPS IN TAKING DICTATION. If taking and transcribing dictation is one of your major jobs, there are a few techniques that can be real time savers for you.

Be ready. The best way to save time and avoid delays is to be ready, always. When your executive calls you is not the time to start looking around for your steno book or sharpening pencils. Have everything ready at all times; if dictation sessions are long, have several pencils sharpened, instead of one. Remember, too, that you are saving the dictator's time by being prepared, something every busy executive appreciates.

Being ready to take dictation at any time does more than save time. If you miss your chance to catch your executive when he has a space in his schedule to dictate, you are making it more difficult for both of you. Here's how one experienced supervisor put it when she was asked about this problem: "Delay a few minutes and he may get on a long distance call or he may be called to another office. You will benefit as much as he by being ready, because if he is pressed for time he will not dictate well, nor will his instructions be as clear as they would have been if you hadn't kept him waiting."

Can you write some of those letters yourself? Does your employer dictate similar replies to certain routine questions week after week? Perhaps you could take over these form style letters and write the answers yourself. This would save your employer the time it takes to dictate the answer and it would save you the double job of taking down notes and then transcribing them.

When you take dictation from more than one person. When you take dictation from several men, you may run into difficulty keeping their letters separate. You can save a lot of time and trouble by keeping separate steno books for each man or by remembering to put the dictator's initials at the end of each letter. This will save you the embarrassment of mixing up correspondence.

Using the rough draft technique to save time. While you are getting used to a new dictator's voice over the dictating machine, you may try making rough drafts of your work. In the long run this can save you time. Instead of wasting good paper while you make your first mistakes, you can make a rough copy on scrap paper or onion skin, correct your errors and type perfect letters. Also, if you have questions you can get the right answers before you type the final copy. Of course, once you become familiar with your employer's dictation methods, you can discard this practice.

When you have to transcribe telegrams in a hurry. What happens when you have three or four telegrams to get out right away, but they are sandwiched in between a batch of letters dictated at the same time? Do you have to leaf through your steno book a page at a time to ferret out the telegrams before you can start typing? Try folding the pages containing telegrams diagonally so that part of the page will extend outside the book. You'll be able to locate your rush work immediately.

Two tricks to cut transcription time. First of all, form a daily schedule. Set aside an hour or so for transcription when interruptions are least likely. You waste a lot of time when you frequently have to stop work and then pick up where you left off.

Try this with your steno book. Take a piece of string about six inches long and fix a button at each end. Stand your steno book between the two buttons and all you have to do is flip the pages.

GOOD LETTER STYLES IN BUSINESS

There are several letter styles that are appropriate for business use. Your employer will probably tell you which ones your company prefers. We are going to discuss the components to the business letter in detail. Therefore, for your convenience, we have placed samples of the five most common styles on the following pages.

HOW TO ADDRESS CORRESPONDENCE. The address is the first step in any business letter and the first place where a beginner can make a mistake.

The address of a letter is very important. In addition to expediting the handling of the letter, a correct address is also a matter of courtesy. A customer or client will not think much of the organization that cannot spell his name right or that omits his business title.

Make sure you have all the necessary information, *before* you start to type. An address includes:

1. the name of the receiver
2. his business title
3. his company name
4. street address
5. city
6. state
7. ZIP Code (which includes zone number)

Prentice-Hall, Inc.

EXECUTIVE OFFICES

Englewood Cliffs, N. J.

WINDSOR 7-1000
AREA CODE 201

July 16, 19 --

Your reference 12:3:1

Miss Sheila Jones
The Modern School for Secretaries
12 Harrington Place
Greenpoint, New York

Dear Miss Jones:

You asked me if there is any one style of setting up a letter that is used more than the others. Probably more business concerns use the block style of letter than any other style, because its marginal uniformity saves time for the typist. Many companies are adopting the full block style, however, as it saves even more time than the block. This letter is an example of the block style.

As you can see, the inside address is blocked and paragraph beginnings are aligned with the left margin, as they are in the full block form. Open punctuation is used in the address.

The date and reference lines are flush with the right margin. The date line is two spaces below the letterhead, and the reference line is two spaces below the date line. The complimentary close begins slightly to the right of the center of the page. Both lines of the signature are aligned with the complimentary close.

I do not advocate including the dictator's initials in the identification line, because his name is typed in the signature.

Sincerely yours,

Martha Scott
Correspondence Chief

mlh

Block Style

Prentice-Hall, Inc.

EXECUTIVE OFFICES

Englewood Cliffs, N. J.

WINDSOR 7-1000
AREA CODE 201

July 16, 19 --

Dear Miss Jones:

Every correspondence manual should include a sample of the official style. It is used in many personal letters written by executives and professional men, and looks unusually well on the executive-size letterhead.

The structural parts of the letter differ from the standard arrangement only in the position of the inside address. The salutation is placed two to five spaces below the date line, depending upon the length of the letter. It establishes the left margin of the letter. The inside address is written in block form, flush with the left margin, from two to five spaces below the final line of the signature. Open punctuation is used in the address.

The identification line, if used, should be placed two spaces below the last line of the address, and the enclosure mark two spaces below that. As the dictator's name is typed in the signature, it is not necessary for the letter to carry an identification line. The typist's initials are on the carbon of the letter, but not on the original.

Sincerely yours,

Martha Scott
Correspondence Chief

Miss Sheila Jones
The Modern School for Secretaries
12 Harrington Place
Greenpoint, New York

Official Style

Prentice-Hall, Inc.

EXECUTIVE OFFICES

Englewood Cliffs, N. J.

WINDSOR 7-1000
AREA CODE 201

July 16, 19 --

Miss Sheila Jones
The Modern School for Secretaries
12 Harrington Place
Greenpoint, New York

Dear Miss Jones:

Most companies have a definite preference as to letter style. Many leading business corporations insist that all letters be typed in semi-block style. This style combines an attractive appearance with utility. Private secretaries, who are not usually concerned with mass production of correspondence, favor it. Here is a sample to add to your correspondence manual.

This style differs from the block form in only one respect--the first line of each paragraph is indented five or ten spaces. In this example the paragraphs are indented ten spaces. As in all letters, there is a double space between paragraphs.

The date line is flush with the right margin, two or four spaces below the letterhead. The complimentary close begins slightly to the right of the center of the page. All lines of the signature are aligned with the complimentary close. Open punctuation is used in the address.

No identification line is used in this example. As the dictator's name is typed in the signature, his initials are not necessary. The typist's initials are shown on the carbon copy.

Very sincerely yours,

Martha Scott
Correspondence Chief

Semi-block Style

Prentice-Hall, Inc.

EXECUTIVE OFFICES

Englewood Cliffs, N. J.

WINDSOR 7-1000
AREA CODE 201

July 16, 19 --

Miss Sheila Jones,
The Modern School for Secretaries,
12 Harrington Place,
Greenpoint, New York

Dear Miss Jones:

This is an example of the indented style of letter. Add this to your correspondence manual along with the other letters I am enclosing.

Many conservative organizations still use the indented style as they prefer it to new forms. The indented style is correct, however, for any type of organization.

Each line of the address is indented five spaces more than the preceding line. The beginning of each paragraph is indented the same as the third line of the address, which is ten spaces. The complimentary close begins a few spaces to the right of the center of the page. Each line of the signature is indented three spaces from the beginning of the complimentary close. Close punctuation is used in the address but not in the signature.

Sincerely yours,

Martha Scott
Correspondence Chief

Enclosures 5

Indented Style

Prentice-Hall, Inc.

EXECUTIVE OFFICES

Englewood Cliffs, N. J.

WINDSOR 7-1000
AREA CODE 201

July 16, 19 - -

Miss Sheila Jones
The Modern School for Secretaries
12 Harrington Place
Greenpoint, New York

Dear Miss Jones:

You have asked me to send you examples of letter styles being used in offices throughout the country.

This letter is an example of the full block style of letter, which has been adopted as a standard at Prentice-Hall. We have reproduced it in our Employee Manual so that everyone will be familiar with the form and the instructions for its use.

Since Prentice-Hall is a leading exponent of modern business methods, they naturally use the most efficient letter form. This style saves time and energy.

As you see, there are no indentations. Everything, including the date and the complimentary close, begins at the extreme left. This uniformity eliminates several mechanical operations in typing letters.

Our dictaphone typists always use this form unless the dictator instructs otherwise. The dictator is at liberty to alter the form if a change is desirable for business reasons.

As the dictator's name is typed in the signature, it is not considered necessary to include his initials in the identification line.

Sincerely,

Martha Scott
Correspondence Chief

cf

Full Block Style

When you start to type. Before you begin to type the inside address on a letter, give some thought to the length of the letter. If the address is not placed correctly, the whole appearance of your page will be thrown off. The address should be indented far enough from the left so that the ensuing message will not look thin and flat. It should be spaced properly from the top so that you do not have to start another page for a relatively short letter. The inside address should be begun between two and twelve spaces from the date line; exactly where is determined by the length of the letter. The address should not extend beyond the middle of the page. Always single space the inside address, even if you plan to double space the rest of the letter.

Here are some other rules for addressing a letter:

Individual and company names: When you are writing to an individual in a company, place the individual's name on the first line, the company's name on the second.

for instance: Mr. Arthur W. Hill
Adams and White Enterprises

Department names: When writing to a particular department in a company, place the company name on the first line, the department name on the second.

Business titles: Business titles or positions are never abbreviated in the address. These include President, Vice-President, Sales Manager, Treasurer, Secretary, and the like. Mr. (or Mrs. or Miss) always goes before the individual's name, even when you use the business title.

When the person has a short business title, such as President, you can put it on the first line following his name. If the title or the name is too long you can place the title on the second line. If this causes the address to run over four lines, you can omit the business title.

for instance: Mr. John A. Jenkins, Manager
Hollingsworth Department Store
4454 East 25 Street
Washington 8, Pennsylvania

Mr. William F. Carter
Business Manager
The Morning Times
477 Allegheny Street
Alton, New Jersey

In this case you should omit the business title.

A title is never hyphenated unless a combination of two offices is being represented, as with Editor-Publisher.

Should you be addressing a man who holds several offices in his company, use the highest office only, unless he signs his letters differently.

Company names: Make sure the company name is exactly as presented on their own letter head. If you haven't a copy of one of their letters, check the telephone directory or call the addressee's office for the correct presentation.

Street address: Never put a sign or a word before the street number in an address.

Correct Form . . . 711 Brisbane Road or 711 Brisbane Road, Apt. 1-A

Incorrect Form . . . #711 Brisbane Road or Apt. 1-A, 711 Brisbane Road

Whether you abbreviate East, West, and the like depends on the length of the line. There are no set rules, so if the line is short, you type out East or West, but if it is long you may use the abbreviated form.

When a street has a numerical name of twelve or under, write it out. With figures over twelve, never place *d, st,* or *th* after the number. Figures are always used for house numbers, with the exception of number one, which is always written out.

for instance: 19 East Ivy Lane, One West 25 Street, 19 - 42 Street

Cities and states: The name of a city is never abbreviated. You may abbreviate states, territories and possessions of the United States but it is not a good practice. Here are the approved abbreviations for states, territories and possessions:

Alabama	AL
Alaska	AK
Arizona	AZ
Arkansas	AR
California	CA
Canal Zone	CZ
Colorado	CO
Connecticut	CT
Delaware	DE
District of Columbia	DC
Florida	FL
Georgia	GA
Guam	GU
Hawaii	HI
Idaho	ID
Illinois	IL
Indiana	IN
Iowa	IA
Kansas	KS
Kentucky	KY
Louisiana	LA
Maine	ME
Maryland	MD
Massachusetts	MA
Michigan	MI
Minnesota	MN
Mississippi	MS
Missouri	MO
Montana	MT
Nebraska	NE
Nevada	NV
New Hampshire	NH
New Jersey	NJ
New Mexico	NM
New York	NY
North Carolina	NC
North Dakota	ND
Ohio	OH
Oklahoma	OK
Oregon	OR
Pennsylvania	PA
Puerto Rico	PR
Rhode Island	RI
South Carolina	SC

South Dakota	SD	Virginia	VA
Tennessee	TN	Washington	WA
Texas	TX	West Virginia	WV
Utah	UT	Wisconsin	WI
Vermont	VT	Wyoming	WY

ZIP Code: The ZIP Code, a five-digit number that includes the zone number of the post office to which the letter is going, follows the state. Be sure to use it if you know it.

for instance: New York, New York 10005

HOW TO USE THE CORRECT FORM OF ADDRESS. Beginners are often confused about which form of address they should use. You'll find this section a handy guide. Here are four rules for addressing a man:

1. Always precede a name by a title (Mr., Dr., Prof., and the like). The only exception is when you have initials indicating degrees or the title Esquire following a name. *Sr., Jr., 3rd,* and *V* or the use of a business position after a name does not take the place of a title.

for instance: Mr. Jeffrey Ashby, V., President

not

Jeffrey Ashby, V., President

2. Initials or abbreviations indicating honors or degrees go after the name of the person addressed, when used. If the person has more than one degree, you would use only the highest. You may use more than one degree, however, if they are in different fields. Never combine a scholastic title and a degree in the same fields. You may use both if the title indicates one field, the degree another.

for instance: Allen P. Davis, Ph.D.

Dr. Peter F. Knight or Peter F. Knight, M.D.

not

Allen P. Davis, A.B., A.M., Ph.D.

Dr. Peter F. Knight, M.D.

3. *Messrs.* may be used in addressing men or men and women of a company, when the names denote individuals. Do not use *Messrs.* as a form of address for corporations or other business organizations that bear impersonal names.

for instance:

Right	*Wrong*
American Manufacturing Company	Messrs. American Manufacturing Company
Messrs. Marvin, Tobin & Smart	Messrs. John Marshal & Sons

4. The term *Esquire* is rare today and is mainly used in addressing well known attorneys. Never place *Esquire* (or the abbreviation *Esq.*, which is also correct) at the beginning of a name, and never use it with another title. The term is strictly masculine and wouldn't be used with a woman's name.

for instance:	Honorable Robert Dane	*not* Honorable Robert Dane, Esq.
	Robert Dane, Esquire	*not* Esquire Robert Dane
	James L. Moran Sr., Esq.	*not* Mr. James L. Moran, Sr., Esq.
	Miss Barbara Cline Attorney at Law	*not* Barbara Cline, Esq.

THE CORRECT FORMS FOR ADDRESSING WOMEN. Since a woman's social position, i.e. single, married, divorced, widowed, determines her title, she is often harder to classify than her male counterpart. Here are eight rules to follow:

1. Should you come across a firm made up of women, either married or unmarried, you would use *Mesdames* or *Mmes.* in the address.

2. An unmarried woman is always addressed as *Miss.* If you aren't sure about her marital status, use *Miss* (*Ms* is sometimes used, but is not widely accepted).

3. A married woman may be addressed in one of two ways:

A. In business, you may use her husband's full name preceded by *Mrs.*, or her given name and married name preceded by *Mrs.* Find out which she prefers, if possible.

for instance: Mrs. James L. Dempsey or
Mrs. Viola Dempsey

B. Socially, you address a woman by her husband's full name preceded by *Mrs.*

4. A widow is addressed in the same fashion as a married woman, both socially and in business.

5. Use the title *Mrs.* rather than *Miss* when addressing a divorcee who has retained her married name. You may use either *Miss* or *Mrs.* if she is using her maiden name. In business she may be addressed by her given name combined with her married name or by both her maiden and married names. Use the form she prefers if you know it. Socially she is addressed by her maiden name combined with her married name. She never uses her ex-husband's given name or initials.

for instance: when husband's name is retained

Business	*Social*
Miss Jane Keane	Mrs. Barth Keane
Mrs. Jane Barth Keane	

when maiden name is used

Business and Social
Mrs. Jane Barth
Miss Jane Barth

6. Never address a married woman by her husband's title.
for instance: Dr. & Mrs. David Bell
or
Mayor & Mrs. Donald Burnett
not Mrs. Dr. John Stone

7. A woman with a professional title should be addressed by her title, followed by her given and last names. A married woman has the option of using her maiden name, if she prefers. In social correspondence you may drop her title if you are addressing her and her husband.

If you aren't sure whether the person you are addressing is male or female, use the masculine form. Women who hold official or honorary positions are addressed as men would be in similar circumstances.

8. Should you be writing to a man and woman in his and her individual capacities, use their respective titles and place one name beneath the other. If they happen to be husband and wife, you may use one line.
for instance: Mrs. Jay R. Cobb / Mr. Stephen R. Lee — Mr. and Mrs. Nathan Cortland

HOW TO SET UP THE REST OF YOUR LETTER. The rest of your letter will fall under seven main headings:

1. The Attention Line
2. The Salutation
3. The Subject Line
4. The Body
5. The Complimentary Close
6. The Signature
7. The Identification Initials

Let's discuss each of these so that all your letters will be perfect in every detail.

Typing the attention line. A business letter is often addressed to a company rather than an individual. When you wish to have the letter delivered to a particular party, you use an *attention line.* This identifies it as a business letter, so that if the addressee is not available, the letter will be opened by someone else.

The attention line should be typed two spaces below the address, preferably flush left, although it can also be centered. The attention line has no punctuation and is not underscored. Use a man's given name or initials in the attention line if you know them. The salutation on a letter with an attention line is always *Gentlemen* as you are addressing the company, not the individual.

for instance: Attention Mr. John F. Light
Attention Mr. Light

Typing the salutation. The salutation is typed two spaces beneath the inside address unless there is an attention line, in which case the salutation is placed two lines below the attention line. Place the salutation flush with the left margin.

When typing the salutation, capitalize the first word, the title and the name, i.e., Dear Mr. Jones: *Dear* is not capitalized if it is not the first word of the salutation.

A colon is always placed at the end of the salutation in a business letter. Commas are used in social letters, especially when they are handwritten.

The salutation form depends on the writer's degree of relationship with the addressee. Your employer will probably tell you which one to use until you come to know his correspondents. With close friends he will undoubtedly use a less formal greeting than with an old and respected client, i.e., Dear Ted: for a close friend, Dear Mr. Adams: for a respected client.

When you are writing to an individual and are not using his name in the salutation, use *Dear Sir.* If the letter is addressed to a corporation, use *Gentlemen.* Never use any titles or other designations with a person's name in the salutation.

Occasionally you may be writing a letter of recommendation, addressed to no one in particular. In this case you say *To Whom It May Concern,* with each word capitalized.

Should you be writing to an organization composed of men and women, it would be perfectly proper to say *Gentlemen* or *Ladies and Gentlemen.* In writing to a man and women, simply say *Dear Sir and Madam;* a married couple would be addressed as *Dear Mr. and Mrs. Smith.*

When you are writing to a woman, never put *Miss* in the salutation unless you use the name, i.e., Dear Miss Smith: not Dear Miss:. *Madam,* however, may be used in a salutation without the name, as *Madam* is also considered a title, i.e., Dear Madam:.

When writing to a firm of women, either *Ladies* or *Mesdames* is acceptable. *Dear* or *My dear* is not used with either of these greetings, i.e., Ladies: not My dear Ladies.

The proper salutation when writing to two women with the same name is:

My dear Mesdames Smith (when they are married)
My dear Misses Smith (when unmarried)
My dear Miss Smith and Mrs. Smith or Ladies (when one is married and one is single)

How to type a subject line. A subject line eliminates the necessity for an involved explanatory sentence at the beginning of the letter. The subject line is flush with the left margin when you employ the full block or simplified letter style. Otherwise it is placed two spaces beneath the salutation and centered.

Remember, the subject line is actually a part of the body of the letter. It is never placed above the salutation.

It is usually better to omit such introductory words as *Re, In Re,* or *Subject,* except in letters concerning legal matters. Place a colon after *Subject* but there is no punctuation after *Re* or *In Re.* The entry should be underscored when you don't use the word *Subject.* Should your entry continue beyond one line, underline the last line only. All important words in the subject line are capitalized.

How to present the body of the letter. When you type the body of a letter, use single spacing unless the letter is very short. Always single space when using half sheet letterheads. Double space between all paragraphs. Should you use the block style, be sure each line is flush with the left margin. For indented or semi-block styles, indent the first line of each paragraph five or ten spaces. Paragraphs are always indented when a letter is double spaced.

Writing dates within letters. You may write the day out or use the figure with the ordinal abbreviation, when the day precedes the month.

for instance: fourth of August or 4th of August

A figure is always used when the month precedes the day, i.e., March 5, 1972 not March Fifth, 1972.

Why uniform spelling is important. There are two accepted spelling forms for many words commonly used in business. Some examples:

inclose, inclosure
enclose, enclosure
indorse, indorsement
endorse, endorsement
inquire, inquiry
enquire, enquiry

Find out which style your company advocates and stick to it. If the company does not have a standard style, you may make your own choice, but be consistent. Don't spell the same word two ways in one letter.

How to type a complimentary close. The complimentary close is typed two spaces below the last line of your letter. With full block style the complimentary close is typed flush with the left margin while with the simplified letter style it is omitted entirely. Place the complimentary close slightly to the right of center with all other letter styles; it should never extend beyond the right margin. If your letter is more than one page, make sure you have at least three lines on the final page before the complimentary close.

Only the first word of the complimentary close is capitalized, and a comma is placed at the end.

The form of the close will generally be determined by your employer. It depends on the relationship between your employer and the addressee. The close and the salutation should match in degree of formality.

Here are some examples of closing and their matching salutations:

	Salutation	Complimentary Close
Formal	Dear Sir:	Very truly yours,
	Dear Madam:	Yours very truly,
	Gentlemen:	Yours truly,
	Mesdames:	Very respectfully yours,
Very Formal	My dear Sir:	Respectfully,
	Sir:	Yours respectfully,
	My dear madam:	Respectfully yours,
	Madam:	Very respectfully yours,
Less Formal	Dear Mr. Elworth:	Sincerely,
	My dear Mr. Elworth:	Sincerely yours,
	Dear Mrs. Gordon:	Yours sincerely,
	My dear Mrs. Gordon:	Very sincerely,
	Dear Miss Lane:	
	My dear Miss Lane:	
Personal	Dear Mr. Allen:	Yours cordially,
	Dear Mrs. Ames:	Cordially,
	Dear Miss Alexander:	Cordially yours,
		Most sincerely,

How to type the signature. Generally the signature on a business letter includes the company name (typed), the signature of the writer, the typed name of the writer and his business title. Type the firm name in capitals, exactly as it is shown on the letterhead. Then make sure the signature is typed precisely as your employer signs his name. Type all business titles and degrees *after* the typed signature. A title is never placed before a written or typed signature, with the exception of *Miss* or *Mrs.*

Many businesses today no longer include the firm's name in the signature as it is usually represented in the letterhead. You may also eliminate the typed name of the writer if this appears in the letterhead.

For a strictly personal letter, do not type in the business title, even if it is typed on a company letterhead.

Letters from attorneys and certified public accountants are generally signed manually, including the firm name. These letters usually express professional opinions or give professional advice.

Where to place the signature. If the firm name is being typed, place it two spaces below the complimentary close. The writer's name is then typed four spaces below the firm's name and the writer's position goes on the same line or on the line beneath. The writer's name and position are placed four lines below the complimentary close when the firm name is not included.

The signature is lined up with the first letter of the complimentary close when the inside address is typed in block form. Line up the signature with the third or fourth letters of the close when the indented form is used for the inside address. In both cases, be sure to block the lines of the signature, unless it would be impractical because of an unusually long line. Never allow a signature line to extend beyond the right-hand margin of the letter.

A woman's signature. A woman's surname should never be preceded only by initials. When initials are used, it is assumed that the writer is a man.

Miss, in parentheses, may precede the signature of a single woman if she wishes. When all titles are omitted, it is assumed that a woman writer is a Miss.

A married woman usually indicates her marital status in her signature, especially on business correspondence. She may place *Mrs.* in parentheses before her typed signature, or her married name may be typed in parentheses beneath her handwritten signature. The latter form is compulsory for social usage only

Widows always sign their names as before their husbands' deaths.

A divorcee uses her given name with her former husband's surname. She may include the initial of her maiden name if she chooses.

When the secretary signs for her boss. Should you sign a letter for your employer, be sure to place your initials directly beneath the signature. If you sign a letter with your own name as secretary to your employer, it is not necessary to include his initials, unless a man in the company has the same name as his. Always make sure that your employer's name is preceded by *Mr.* or whatever his title is.

for instance: Secretary to Mr. Hanlan

not

Secretary to Mr. C. J. Hanlan

or

Secretary to C. J. Hanlan

What to do with indentification initials. Unless your company has a different policy, put your initials on the carbon copies only This is your company's record of who typed it. The dictator's initials are omitted as his name is typed in the signature. Sometimes the person who dictates the letter is not the one who is going to sign it. In this case put down the initials of the signer first, follow with the dictator's initials, and finally the transcriber's.

When you are employing the usual identification line, start typing flush with the left margin and one space below the closing line. The typist's initials may be lower case while the others are in caps. A colon is usually placed between sets of initials although some firms may prefer the use of a diagonal.

► **Timesaving Hint.** Keep your supplies up to date. When your employer is ready to dictate, you should be ready too. Have your desk well stocked with necessary stationery. Set a time each week to replenish your supplies. And, don't be a supply borrower: you'll be disliked fast.

TYPING STATISTICAL MATERIAL

You will not run into statistical typing too often, but when you do, don't panic or become careless. Beginners are either scared to death by the idea of a statistical report or else don't give it much thought at all and throw it together in a careless manner. Remember—the tabulation on a statistical report must be accurate, neat, easy to read and attractive to the eye. Here are some tips on how to manage it.

How to center a heading. First, find the center of your paper, using the numbered scale in front of the platen. Most scales run from zero to one hundred and twenty. With the basic page measuring 8½ by 11 inches and the left edge of the paper on zero, your mid-point would be around fifty.

If for some reason you aren't using zero as the left edge, there is another way to center. Let's say left edge of the paper is at 20 on the scale and the right edge at 120, giving you a span of 100. Divide this by 2, and add the result (50) to the left margin (20) and the answer, 70, is the center point on your paper.

Now to center a heading, add all the letters, spaces and punctuation marks in the heading and divide by two. Assume you have a total of 58, which, when divided by 2, leaves 29. Backspace 29 times from the center point and you are ready to start typing. If you have an uneven total, drop one and work with the even number.

Spacing a table. A table must be carefully spaced to be neat and attractive. With a little practice you will be able to set up tables with little more effort than it takes to write a letter.

Sometimes you will have a short table to be incorporated in a letter or report rather than put on a separate sheet. When this happens, use these spacing rules:

1. Leave three line spaces between the main title and subheading.
2. Leave at least two spaces between subheadings and column headings.
3. Leave at least two spaces between the column headings and the items in the columns.
4. With a short table, you may double space the items. However, it is better to single space the items rather than have the table run over to another page.

On occasion you will have to set up a table on a separate page. First you must determine how many line spaces are available before figuring the vertical spacing. Of course, the length of the paper will decide the number of lines. The basic rule is—six line spaces equal one inch. Therefore, the standard 8½ by 11 inch sheet has sixty-six lines. Here is the way you would center your table vertically on the page:

1. Add up the number of lines in your tabulation.
2. Add to this total the number of blank lines that you are going to leave between the typed lines. These include the blank lines between title and column headings and also the lines between the column headings and the columns themselves.
3. Subtract the total number of lines from the total number of line spaces on the page.
4. Divide the answer by two and you will have the number of line spaces left at the top and bottom of the page.
5. When your table is going to run over to a second page, plan your first page so that you won't have only one item to carry over. You should have at least four to six entries on the second sheet. Always retype the column headings on the second page when you have a two page table.

Tip for horizontal spacing. The first thing you have to note is how wide your paper is and how many characters you'll be able to put on a line. One way to do this is to simply read the number of units your paper spans on the typewriter scale. If the left edge cuts the scale at 15 and the right edge hits 115, subtract 15 from 115 and you have 100 spaces to work with.

Another way to determine horizontal spacing is by the following formula: ten spaces of pica type equal 1 inch and twelve spaces of elite type equal one inch. A piece of paper 8½ by 11 inches would therefore have 85 spaces of pica type and 102 spaces of elite type.

When you have to set up a table. A four column table is perhaps the simplest tabular exercise. Let's use the one illustrated below for our example:

Employee Automobile Identification List
1972-1973

Year	*Make*	*Model*	*Owner*
1971	Ford	Sedan	Alexander, John
1970	Chevrolet	Station Wagon	Barton, Elaine
1967	Dodge	Hardtop	Benton, James
1968	Cadillac	Sedan	Dane, Robert
1972	Pontiac	Hardtop	Doyle, Alice
1969	Buick	Sedan	Franklin, Herbert
1968	Plymouth	Sedan	Harding, Ralph
1972	Volkswagen	Sedan	Jansen, Arnold

Follow this step by step procedure:

1. Count up the number of characters in the widest entry in each column.
2. Decide on the number of spaces you will have between columns. Let us say you decide on seven for our example.
3. Add the number of figures in the columns and the number of spaces between the columns; in our case we would come up with 64. Assuming we are using an 8½ by 11 inch page with 102 spaces across, we would subtract 64 from 102 and get 38. This is the number of spaces you have for your margins.
4. Divide the 38 spaces in half so you have equal margins of 19 spaces on the left and 19 on the right.
5. Now you set up your margins and tab stops. Our table will be arranged like this:
   A. The left margin is set at 19 on the typewriter scale.
   B. Set the first tab stop at 30 (Four characters in the first column plus 7 spaces between column 1 and 2, added to original 19 space margin).
   C. The second tab stop goes at 48 (Eleven characters in longest item of second column [Thunderbird] plus seven spaces between column 2 and 3, added on to 30 = 48).
   D. Third tab stop goes at 66 (Eleven characters in longest term in third column [convertible] plus seven spaces between column 3 and 4, added to 48 = 66).

► **Hint.** When setting up your tab figures, make up a diagram like this one and avoid wasting time with constant recounting.

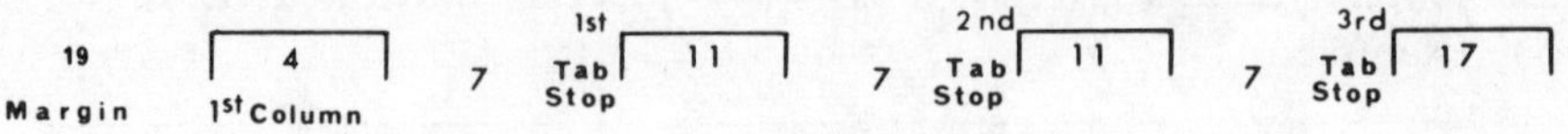

How to set up a table with a stub. A *stub* is a descriptive column on the left side of a table. Items following the stub are known as *descriptive items, side headings,* or *particulars.* Use the same method for horizontal spacing as described on page 67, unless you have a complicated table. When this occurs your best bet is to type a rough draft, estimating the spacing. Use the following suggestions:

1. Decide on a left margin that will be compatible with your table.
2. Type the longest side heading in the table first.
3. Follow across the page, spacing for the widest figures in each column. Estimate the number of spaces to be left between columns. On the rough draft you will find it easier if you substitute *x's* for the real figures. For instance, $3,767,576.77 becomes $x,xxx,xxx.xx. You are only interested in spacing right now, not the actual figures.

   Leave in commas, dollar signs, decimal points and per cent signs to keep spacing accurate. At this point your rough draft would look like this:

   Total sales $xxx,xxx.xx $xxx,xxx.xx $xxx,xxx.xx $xxx,xxx.xx

4. Leave enough space at the top so you can easily arrange your column headings.

   for instance:

	San Francisco Office	West Johnstown Office	Kansas City Office	New York Office
Total sales	**$xxx,xxx.xx**	**$xxx,xxx.xx**	**$xxx,xxx.xx**	**$xxx,xxx.xx**

5. If your first draft doesn't work out, you can make the necessary adjustments at a glance and then go on to the final typing.

When you have to type a financial statement. You may be called upon at one time or another to type a financial statement for your employer. The most important thing to remember is that a financial statement must be presented so the figures are easily understood. The best way to do this is to follow the procedure outlined below:

1. List all assets on the left side of the sheet; list all liabilities on the right side.

2. When an item is too long to fit on one line, it is carried over to a second or third line. See illustration—"Less Accrued Depreciation."

3. The subtraction of depreciation from plant and equipment value is shown in a separate column to the left of the main column. This separate column has its own dollar sign before the first figure. Draw a line beneath this column to show the end of the example, and the result is typed out in the main column on the same line as the last item of the inner column.

4. Leaders (. . . . .) should be used between the items and the main column. They should never be used between the inner column and the main column.

5. Show the total under "Liabilities" directly opposite the total under "Assets." The line before the total under "Liabilities" is immediately above the figures.

6. You do not have to write the word "Total" when the figure is obviously a total.

► **Note.** Should the figures in your table all end in three or even six zeros, it would be simpler for you to drop the zeros and mark the table: "figures in thousands" or "figures in hundreds of thousands." Be sure you have your employer's permission, however, before adopting this idea.

GENERAL BALANCE SHEET, DECEMBER 31, 19—

Assets			*Liabilities*	
Cash		$ 600	Accounts Payable	$ 1,500
Marketable Securities		2,200	Preferred Stock	16,000
Accounts Receivable		5,200	Common Stock	16,000
Inventories		8,000	Profit & Loss Surplus	3,200
Plant & Equipment	$12,000		Contingency Reserve	200
Less Accrued Depreciation	2,000	10,000		
Investments		1,300		
Patents & Good Will		9,600		
		$36,900		$36,900

How to align figures in a column. This is a relatively simple task until you have numbers of different values. Here's what to do when you run into this problem.

1. *Columns of whole numbers are aligned on the right.*

```
     15
    550
  9,999
777,954
```

2. *Figures with decimal points are aligned by the decimal points.*

```
  .7
 1.4
36.5
 7.598
  .46
```

3. *With a column of dissimilar figures, you may align them on the left or center them.*

715	$85
4321	35 ounces
39½	14 gross
$60	41.7%
44 lbs.	

Where to place the dollar sign and other symbols in a column. Dollar signs, plus and minus signs, per cent symbols, and the like are always aligned in a column.

The dollar sign is placed in front of the first figure in the column and in front of totals and subtotals in columns containing only dollar figures. Align the dollar marks with the widest figure in the column, regardless of whether the widest figure is the first in the column.

```
$    88.00
    987.46
 11,148.32
    391.87
----------
$12,615.65
```

Place the dollar sign before the first number in the column when you have a column of dollar figures and the first spaces of the column are blank. Never put the dollar sign at the top of the column in a situation like this.

```
________
________
________
$9875.14
```

When you have double columns of figures in a single money column, put the dollar sign before both figures in the first line.

Repair Expense	$1,000	-	$1,400
Replacement Expense	2,200	-	3,500

Sometimes you will have a column of numbers where some are monetary figures and some are not. In this case place a dollar sign before each monetary figure. The dollar signs are aligned with the longest dollar figure.

```
     1,849
$    2,100
        71%
     8,000
$798,431
       616
$  71,900
```

How to type leaders. Those periods connecting the stubs to the first column are known as leaders. They should be typed at every other space because a solid line of periods looks dark and unattractive. In order to keep the periods vertically aligned, decide at the beginning whether you wil type them as odd or even numbers on your typewriter scale. Then be sure to begin all your leaders on the odd or even number.

The leader always stops at least two or three spaces before the start of the longest figure. All leaders end at the same point.

Leaders are never used between columns of figures. They are only used between the stub and first column.

When the side heading is written on more than one line, do not use leaders after the first line. They are placed only after the second line.

Hyphens are never substituted for leaders. When figures are involved, they can easily be mistaken for minus signs.

TYPING SHORT CUTS FOR THE NEW SECRETARY

A new secretary often wastes a lot of time on unnecessary motions when she is typing, simply because she isn't aware of the tricks of the trade. If you want to turn out work like a veteran, try applying the following suggestions.

How to chain feed. When you have a series of cards to type, you can save a lot of time by typing the first card and then feeding backwards until the card has a top margin of about three-quarters of an inch. Place the next card so that the bottom will be held in place by the first card. Each succeeding card will be held in place by the one preceding it, and the cards will fall in the same order that they are typed.

The same system can also be used for envelopes, saving you the chore of re-sorting. Occasionally you will have envelopes that are too thick to feed from the front. When this happens, try chain feeding from the back of the platen. To do this place the next envelope to be typed between the first envelope and the paper table before removing the first. A single turn of the platen pops out one envelope and automatically puts the next one in place. You should prepare a chain of three before you start to type your first envelope. Make certain that the flaps are open before inserting the envelope into the machine. This makes insertion easier and produces a more even type.

How to type postcards. It is possible for you to type the address and the message without turning the card by hand. First, type one side of the card; then turn the platen quickly and the card will pop out and fall back against the paper table and drop into place behind the platen. Another turn of the platen and you are ready to start typing.

You might try giving the platen an extra quick twirl when you are finished typing the card. In this fashion you can sail the card over the top of your machine and into a receiving basket.

How to type above and below the line. Chemical formulas, degrees in temperature or references to footnotes are a few instances where you have to use the ratchet detent lever, or "automatic line finder." "Line position reset" is another name for this device. You can revolve the platen freely to any position through use of this lever, and when you are finished the platen can be returned to the same spacing position at which you were originally typing.

The variable line spacer is another operation entirely. While it allows you to revolve the platen freely, it will not return automatically to the same relative spacing position.

How to sandwich in rush jobs. Suppose your boss dashes up to your desk with a telegram or memo and says "Please get this out right away. Make an original and two copies." Most beginners immediately rip out whatever is in their typewriters and then start on the rush work. When they are finished they have the unpleasant and time consuming task of re-aligning their original work.

There is a much faster and simpler way:

1. Back feed the machine until you have a two inch margin left on the work you are presently typing. Use your ratchet detent lever for this operation.
2. Place the first sheet of your telegram against the paper table, behind the material that is already in the machine.
3. Place clean sheets behind each sheet of carbon being used for the work already in your typewriter. This process gives you your carbon copies of the telegram or memo. It also prevents the rush work from becoming imprinted on your original letters. Should your telegram require more carbons than you already have in the machine, simply add the necessary number in the usual manner.

4. Turn the platen until your telegram is in the typing position and then return the ratchet detent lever to its normal position.
5. After you have finished typing the telegram, back feed until the telegram can easily be removed. Remove the carbon backing sheets and forward feed the original work to the point where you stopped and you are ready to continue.

This is much simpler than it sounds and you will find it infinitely better than trying to re-align five or ten carbons that have been removed from your typewriter.

Cut time with carbons. Beginners are usually very meticulous about carbons. They fit them neatly together and then have to separate the finished copies one at a time. Instead of all this fuss, why not cut one corner off the top of your carbon sheets and then set up your carbons so they protrude slightly from the bottom of the writing paper. When you are finished typing, simply hold the top corner of your letter with one hand (where you cut off the carbon), hold the bottoms of the carbons with the other hand, and separate. Some brands of carbon already have their corners cut for just this reason.

Occasionally you may want to type red figures or letters in the carbon copy of a report. This can be accomplished without removing the report from the typewriter. All you have to do is insert a piece of red carbon at the desired spot, type the figures, remove the red carbon and continue typing.

If you want to prevent onion-skin paper from creasing or "treeing" with carbon lines, just add a sheet of heavy paper to the back of the carbon pack before you insert it in the typewriter.

Keep carbon paper away from direct sunlight and heat.

When you have to type on carbon copies only. When you want to place a special message on the carbon copies that you don't want to appear on the original, insert a small scrap of paper over the original letter and start typing. If you don't want the message to appear on all carbons, place an additional scrap of paper in front of each copy you want to remain clear.

You may be able to keep even your first page free of indentations when you are typing these messages on the carbons, with one of the following systems:

(a) *If the message will go at the top of the carbons:*

1. Insert the paper into the typewriter in usual manner.
2. Free the paper by disengaging the paper release lever.
3. Move the carbon back an inch or so above the original.
4. Return the paper release lever to tight position.
5. Feed the material back and type in the information.
6. Feed the material forward again.

7. Align the original with the carbon pack by using the paper release lever. Put the paper release lever in tight position and you are all set to type your letter.

(b) *If the message will go at the bottom of the carbons:*

1. Position the machine to exactly where you want the information to appear.
2. Disengage the paper release lever.
3. The original can now be slipped out of the machine without disturbing the rest of the pack. Now engage the paper release lever and start typing.

► **Warning.** Don't forget to line up the pack to the exact typing position you want *before* removing the original. The original is your only guide to the sheets beneath the carbon.

When you have to insert numerous sheets. Some machines are equipped with special devices to accommodate large packs of paper, but what do you do when your machine doesn't have one? Beginners have been known to type the same letter twice because they couldn't fit all the carbons in the typewriter. Here are some methods you can use to avoid this extra work.

It is easy to insert several sheets with carbons when you place them beneath the flap of an envelope.

When you have a medium size pack of paper, gather the sheets together and insert them at the back of the platen *without* the carbon. Roll your platen just enough to hold the paper securely in place. Now insert your carbons one at a time, with the shiny side facing you. Then just roll the pack into position and type.

You may use this system with printed forms as it keeps them properly aligned.

A very large pack of paper and carbons demands special treatment, therefore, you will find this device most effective.

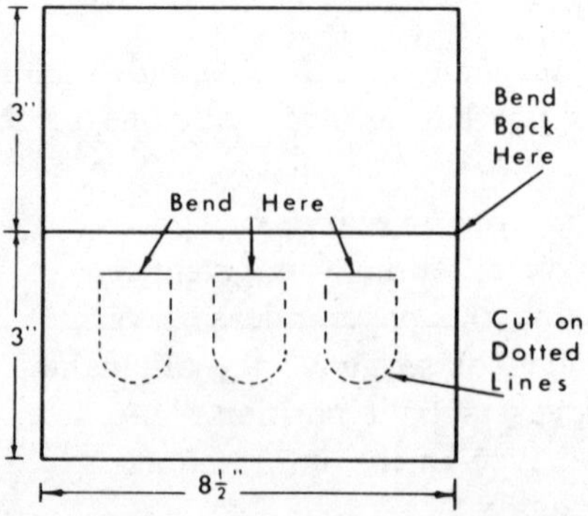

Take an 8½ by 6 inch strip of flimsy Manila tag and fold it down the center, lengthwise. About one-half inch from the crease, cut three U-shaped slots across the upper half of the folded strip. Lift up and bend backward the tongues formed by the slots. Then insert the assembled sheets of paper into the folded strip. Feed the tongues from the U-slots into the typewriter. You will find that the platen grasps them more readily than it does a thick pack of paper. Be sure to remove the folded strip before you begin to type.

When you have to type on printed forms. Always check the alignment on printed forms by holding them up to the light before beginning to type. Place all the forms in the typewriter *without* the carbon paper, just enough to hold them in alignment, and then use the method described in the previous section for the insertions.

When you have to draw lines. When you want to draw a vertical line, first release the platen by using either the variable line spacer or the ratchet detent lever. Roll the platen up while holding a pencil (or ball point pen) firmly in the fork of the ribbon guide at the desired spot, not through the ribbon.

For a horizontal line you follow the same procedure, except that instead of releasing the platen and rolling it up, you use the carriage release and allow the carriage to move across the paper until the line is completed.

Horizontal lines may be easily drawn with an underscore, if you have an electric machine with an automatic underscore key. It takes too much time to underscore on a manual typewriter, especially if you have several lines to draw.

Typing tabular material. The tabulating device on your typewriter is not solely for statistical typing. Learn how to use it to cut down the time consumed with your everyday typing chores.

For example, since most of your letters will be of the same approximate length, you can set a tab stop for the date line, which will also serve for the complimentary close and signature, unless you are using full block style. You may also set another stop for your paragraph indentation.

These may seem like trivial suggestions but when you total up the seconds you spend spacing for these items on each letter, you will find the minutes stretch into hours during one month's time. Use all the little shortcuts you can find and you'll be surprised at how much time can be saved.

Making special characters not on your machine. You can combine standard characters to form special characters that may not be on your keyboard. Here are some examples:

¶	paragraph mark	P and l
÷	division sign	colon and hyphen
£	Pound Sterling sign	f and t, or L and f
ç	Cedilla beneath "c"	c and comma
!	exclamation point	apostrophe and period
=	equation sign	Hyphen--use ratchet detent lever and turn platen slightly
[]	brackets	underscore and diagonal

When you are typing small labels. Use this system and you will be able to type labels with both hands instead of holding the label with one hand and typing with the other.

1. Make a horizontal pleat about an inch deep in a sheet of paper.
2. Place sheet of paper in machine in usual manner, keeping the pleat so the folded edge will be up when the material is in a writing position. The pleat will form a pocket.
3. Insert the label when the pocket appears at the front of your platen. You may be able to line up several labels side by side.
4. Feed all the material back so that you can type on the label.

When you want to have the same number of lines on each page. If you have a typewriter with a numbered strip at the left edge of the platen, try the following:

1. Feed each page into the typewriter with the number one on the platen strip.
2. Take note of the number at which you begin typing the first line on your model page. Be sure to start all pages on the same number.
3. Check the number on which you type your last line. Finish all pages on the same number.

Here is another way to make sure you have the same number of lines on each page.

1. Type your first sheet.
2. Indicate the first line on the next sheet by placing a pencil mark in line with the bottom edge of the first line of type, so you can align your machine on the mark.
3. About four lines before the final line of type, make a second pencil mark, so you can see the mark as it comes out of the carriage. Then you know you have four lines left to type on the page.

6. HOW TO SEND TELEGRAMS AND CABLES

When your employer says "Take a telegram, Miss Smith," do you write it down, dash it off on the typewriter and send it out without any further thought? If so, you could be wasting money. There are different kinds of telegraphic service, some less expensive than others. Sometimes there is a better way. The charts and information in this chapter are set up to give you instant answers on how to dispatch your telegrams and cables efficiently and economically.

WHY SEND A TELEGRAM? The principle advantages of a telegram are three:

1. It is sent and delivered quickly.
2. Unlike a telephone call, a telegram provides a written record of your message, through the carbon copy of the blank you type.
3. You can send a telegram to a place where your party hasn't arrived yet with the assurance he will get it as soon as he appears.

This does not mean, however, that you send a telegram at the drop of a hat. Telegrams in abundance can run into quite a bit of money. Consider the following factors before you decide on a telegram.

1. Letters are definitely cheaper than telegrams. Will the time saved compensate for the extra cost of the telegram? Another more important question: Will your telegram actually save time? When you are sending a message late on a Friday afternoon, chances are it will not be delivered until Monday morning. A letter would probably get there just as fast, so why pay extra? If your employer wants to have the telegram delivered at the recipient's home on a Saturday, you're justified in paying the additional charges, but this will be unusual. Naturally, you should check with your employer before using a letter instead of a telegram.

2. Would a telephone call be more economical than a telegram? When a message requires a reply it is sometimes better to make a long distance call. Suppose you are sending a message that demands an immediate answer from one of the company's branch managers. If the total cost of one long distance telephone call would be around two dollars, the cost of two telegrams could be well over three dollars. Why not take advantage of the savings, and save time besides?

KINDS OF TELEGRAPH SERVICE AVAILABLE. Domestic telegraph service connects all points served by wire in the continental United

States, Mexico, Canada, Saint Pierre and Miquelon Islands. Domestic service offers three classes of telegrams: fast telegrams, day letters, and night letters. They differ in speed and in cost. Once you have decided to use a telegram, you must determine which class will serve your purpose best.

1. Fast Telegram. This is the most expensive service available on a cost per word basis. You are charged a flat rate for fifteen words, and there is no discount if your message runs less. You are charged extra for every word over the fifteen mark, but the address and signature are not counted as words, and you may use code. Of course, this is also the fastest service available. It only takes one hour to send a telegram from New York City to Los Angeles, California.

2. Day Letter. A day letter costs less per word than a fast telegram, but the minimum wordage is fifty words, so the flat rate is actually higher. Over the fifty word limit you are charged extra for each group of five words. Under this plan fifty-two words would count as fifty-five and fifty-eight words would count as sixty.

A fifty word day letter costs approximately forty per cent more than the initial charge for a fast telegram. Let's say the charge for a fifteen word telegram is $1.70; a day letter would cost about $2.40. But for that extra 70¢ you can send three times the amount of words. Again, code may be used, and the address and signature are not counted as words.

A day letter takes an hour or so longer to reach its destination than a fast telegram.

3. Night Letter. This is the least expensive service, by any measurement. The flat rate is for a minimum of fifty words, with each additional group of five words costing extra. If the rate for a fast telegram to a specified city is $1.40, the night letter would cost you only about $1.00.

Delivery may be on the morning of the following day (next *business* day for a business message). You have until 2:00 A.M. to file a night letter with the telegraph company. When you have a message that can wait until the next morning, your savings will be considerable. You don't save any money by cutting a night letter to less than fifty words; the basic rate remains the same.

HOW DO YOU DECIDE WHICH CLASS TO USE? Your choice will be the class that satisfies your speed requirements at the least cost.

• *The time factor.* When sending a telegram across the country you must not forget the variations of the time zones. There are four time zones in the United States—Eastern, Central, Mountain, and Pacific. Let us suppose you are in Los Angeles; it is three o'clock in the afternoon and you want to send a fast message to New York City. With the three hour time difference, plus normal delivery time, a telegram would not arrive at its destination until seven in the evening. Since the message wouldn't be read until the following morning, you could obtain the same results with a night letter for far less money.

Before you send any telegram check the table below. It shows the standard time in each of the zones when it is 12 o'clock Eastern Standard Time, and which major cities fall within each zone.

Eastern Time	12:00 o'clock
Central Time	11:00 A.M.
Mountain Time	10:00 A.M.
Pacific Time	9:00 A.M.

Time Belt of Principal Cities

Albany	Eastern	Minneapolis	Central
Atlanta	Eastern	Mobile	Central
Baltimore	Eastern	New Orleans	Central
Boston	Eastern	New York	Eastern
Buffalo	Eastern	Omaha	Central
Chicago	Central	Philadelphia	Eastern
Cincinnati	Eastern	Pittsburgh	Eastern
Cleveland	Eastern	Portland, Oreg.	Pacific
Denver	Mountain	Providence	Eastern
Detroit	Eastern	Richmond	Eastern
Galveston	Central	Rochester, N.Y.	Eastern
Indianapolis	Central	St. Louis	Central
Jackson, Miss.	Central	San Antonio	Central
Jacksonville	Eastern	Seattle	Pacific
Kansas City, Mo.	Central	Springfield, Mass.	Eastern
Los Angeles	Pacific	Tampa, Fla.	Eastern
Louisville	Central	Toledo	Eastern
Memphis	Central	Washington, D. C.	Eastern
Milwaukee	Central		

► **Remember.** Daylight Saving Time is one hour ahead. It can either increase or decrease the time differential, depending upon which zone is on Standard and which is on Daylight Saving Time.

for instance: New York (Eastern Zone) is on Daylight Saving Time, while San Francisco (Pacific Zone) is on Standard Time. Therefore, the difference is increased from three to four hours.

Los Angeles (Pacific Zone) is on Daylight Saving Time, while Chicago (Central Zone) is on Standard Time. Therefore, the time difference is decreased to only one hour.

When both New York and San Francisco are on Daylight Saving Time, the difference remains at the normal three hours.

• *How many words do you need?* Remember, it doesn't take many words to turn a fast telegram into an expensive proposition. If your message is a long one, you may *have* to sacrifice speed for economy, and use a day or night letter.

Don't use a word unless it is essential to the meaning of your sentence. Most of the time words like *the, a,* and *to* can be dropped without any loss of clarity. Take the following example of unnecessary verbosity:

AM ATTENDING TO BUSINESS IN LOS ANGELES
FOR THE NEXT FEW DAYS STOP WILL YOU WIRE ME
WHEN THE MATERIAL ABOUT THE HODGES ACCOUNT
IS COMPLETED STOP REGARDS TO EVERYONE.

(Total - 30 words)

Here is the same message written well within the fifteen word limit without any loss of meaning:

ATTENDING BUSINESS IN LA TILL 1/25. WIRE
ME WHEN HODGES ACCOUNT MATERIAL COMPLETED.
REGARDS.

(Total - 14 words)

The important thing to remember in composing your telegrams is that nouns, verbs and adjectives are the important words. "Stop" may sound very glamorous and professional, but it is chargeable; the plain old period is free.

HOW TO DETERMINE THE COST OF YOUR TELEGRAM. You may compute the basic rates for the class of message and the additional charge for extra words by using the charts supplied by Western Union. Confusion often surrounds several points, however, including the following:

1. Addresses. There is no charge for the essential material in the address. "Personal" and "Will Call" are free notations. You will be charged, however, for alternate names or addresses.

2. Signature and address of sender. There is no charge for the name of the sender. Included free of charge in the date line are the city and state from which the telegram is sent. However, there will be a charge for the sender's street address if you wish to include it. In the signature you may include the company name and the name of the sender. If the sender's department within the organization is indicated, however, there will be an extra charge. Identifying titles are also chargeable.

3. States, counties, cities. The names of states, counties, and cities are counted according to the number of words they contain. For instance, "San Francisco" is two words; "New York City" three. Running the names together as in "Newyorkcity" will not affect the count.

When names are abbreviated, they count as one word. For example, LA is one word.

► **Note.** This differs from international service (see below) where names of cities and streets may be run together and counted as one word.

4. **Abbreviations.** Abbreviations containing no more than five letters are counted as one word. They should be typed without spaces or periods—AFL, FOB, NAM.

5. **Initials.** Initials are considered separate words if they are separated by spaces. When written without spaces, the count is one word for every five letters or fraction thereof. Therefore, G S is counted as two words, but GS is one word.

6. **Personal names.** The count for personal names is determined by the way they are written. Van der Long would count as three words; Van Long, as two words; and O'Casey, as one word.

7. **Mixed groups of letters and figures.** Mixed groups of letters, figures, and the characters $, /, &, #, ′ (indicating minutes or feet), and ″ (indicating inches or seconds) are counted at the rate of five characters, or fraction thereof, to the word in messages between points in the United States and between points in Mexico. Therefore, "four thousand" is counted as two words but 4000 is counted as one word; $77.67 is one word (the decimal is not counted); 64F4B, as one word, but 2000th (six characters) is counted as two words.

► **Note.** Each figure, affix, dash, sign, and bar in a group is counted as a word in messages sent to Canada, Saint Pierre and Miquelon Islands.

8. **Punctuation marks.** You will not be charged for punctuation marks and quotation marks, but the *words* "Stop", "comma", and the like count as one word each.

9. **Compound words.** Compound words that are hyphenated in the dictionary will be counted as one word. This includes such terms as "mother-in-law". When two or more words are combined which are not listed as combinations in the dictionary, they are counted individually.

HOW MANY COPIES DO YOU NEED? Most companies require you to make four copies of a telegram, although some may demand more or less. Under the four copy plan, the original copy is for pickup by the telegraph messenger. A second copy is generally sent by mail for confirmation purposes. The other two copies are used for filing, one to the general file and the other to the telegraph account file to be used for bookkeeping.

► **Hint.** Mail your confirmation copy right away. This prevents the recipient from saying he never received the message, and it also serves as a check on the telegram's transmission.

RULES FOR TYPING TELEGRAMS. When you have to send a telegram, keep the following rules in mind:

1. You will find one box in each corner of the telegraph blank. Be sure to check either "Domestic Service" or "International Service." Don't forget to include the class of service two spaces above the address.
2. The date and hour should be typed in the upper right corner, two spaces above the address.
3. The salutation and complimentary close are omitted.
4. Double space the message. You may use paragraphs.
5. Never divide words at the end of a line.
6. In the appropriate space on the blank, type "Pd" (for Paid) or "Collect." Unless it is already printed on the blank, type the address and telephone number of the sender in the lower left-hand corner of the blank. You may also place reference initials here, if you use them.
7. When the telegram is to be charged, type the name of the charge account in the space provided on the blank.
8. There are markings for special use. Should you be sending a telegram in reply to a message, but do not know the address of the sender, type "Answer date" or "Answer" after the name of the addressee, and send the telegram to the city and telegraph office from which the original telegram came. You can identify the telegraph office at point of origin by one or two letters which may appear immediately preceding the "place from" in the date line of the telegram received.
9. You can indicate that an answer is requested by typing "AR" in the space provided for payment information.
10. The chargeable words "Report Delivery" written as part of the address will bring a collect telegram back to your office indicating when and to whom the telegram was delivered.

SOME OTHER THINGS YOU CAN DO THROUGH TELEGRAPHIC SERVICE. Your telegraph company provides several unusual services for the executive's convenience. Have you been overlooking them?

Sending the same message to multiple addresses. You can send the same message to a number of people. In this case, you only have to type the text of the telegram once. Then list the names and addresses of the recipients on a piece of paper or on forms provided by Western Union for this purpose. At the top of the list type "Please send the attached message to the following 7 (or other number) addresses."

Sending a telegram to a person on a train. The telegram is always sent in care of the conductor. It is forwarded to a point where the train is scheduled to stop, and is delivered from there.

Include the following information when sending a telegram of this nature:

1. the name of the passenger
2. the train name or number and the direction in which it is traveling
3. car and reservation number
4. station and arrival time
5. city and state

Sending a telegram to a person on a plane. Messages of this type are sent to an airport to be delivered when the plane lands. Give the following information:

1. name of the passenger
2. the flight number and direction in which the plane is traveling
3. airport and arrival time
4. city and state

Messages cannot be delivered to a plane passenger while the plane is in flight.

Direct wire service. You can send a telegram direct to the Western Union office by means of a machine called "Desk-Fax." This saves delivery time and eliminates the possibility for error in giving the message to Western Union over the phone. The Desk-Fax also receives incoming telegrams direct from Western Union. To transmit a message you simply type it on a special form and slip it onto the revolving drum of the facsimile machine. The Desk-Fax at the Western Union office prints a picture of the telegram automatically and it is immediately dispatched.

Errand service. You may use telegraph messengers for a wide variety of errands, including:

Business errands. Envelopes, documents, blueprints, advertising cuts, press releases, and the like can be picked up and delivered by this service.

Personal errands. Forgotten articles from home or office, garments from the tailor, prescriptions to the pharmacist, notes, gifts, and so on can all be handled by a Western Union messenger.

Gift deliveries. This covers delivery of such items as flowers, perfume, candy, cigars, and so on for birthdays, weddings, and similar occasions.

General errands. You can also hire messengers to act as temporary employees, as guides for visitors, and as intracity couriers.

The errand service is available either on a trip or on an hourly basis.

HOW TO SEND CABLEGRAMS AND RADIOGRAMS. Messages to foreign countries must be sent over cable or radio facilities. Basic procedures are similar to those for sending telegrams. Cablegrams and radiograms can be filed with Western Union for transmittal to any of the international carriers, or you can file directly with the carriers themselves. When you wish a message to go to a specific carrier but are filing with Western Union, be sure to type the name of the desired route directly after the destination. Western Union then forwards it to the proper carrier for transmission.

The Fast Rate Message (FR). This is the fastest service for international use. It parallels the fast telegram in domestic service. The distance traveled determines the minimum charge, but you will seldom have to pay more than 34 cents per word. The minimum charge is for seven words. International service charges for the address and signature.

Letter Telegrams (LT). Sometimes known as Cable Letters or Radio Letters, these provide an overnight service that will handle messages of some length when there is no great urgency. Plain language, not code, must be used but a registered code address or signature may be employed. The charges are one-half those for the fast message, since slower service is involved. Charges are assessed for a minimum of twenty-two words. Again address and signature are charged for, as is the indicator "LT" (for Letter Telegram) which must be inserted immediately preceding the address. A letter telegram is deferred in transmission to all other traffic. Generally, overnight service is available except in Australia, New Zealand, the Far East, the Middle East, and some countries in the Near East. The countries in these areas set their own limits on delivery of LT's. Western Union is always happy to answer any questions you may have concerning this service.

Shore to Ship Radio. A radiogram may be sent to a person aboard a ship at sea. The following information must be given in the address:

1. the name of the passenger
2. the ship
3. the radio station

A shore-to-ship message can be sent only as a fast radiogram; therefore, code may be used. The signature and the address are included in the chargeable word count, but terms such as "Newyorkradio" may be run together to count as one word.

THE INTERNATIONAL TIME CHARTS. As with telegrams you should always check the time at your destination before sending an overseas wire. The chart below was compiled by the American Cable & Radio Corporation and will do much to simplify your task. Don't forget you can gain or lose a day in crossing, the International Date Line. Therefore, your computations may take you into yesterday and tomorrow.

WHEN SHOULD YOU USE A TIME CHART? Every time you send a wire you should consult the time chart. Take the following example:

It is one o'clock in the afternoon in your office in Indianapolis. You are sending a message to a manufacturer in Le Havre, France. A fast cablegram is the first thing that pops into your head, but on checking the time chart you discover the following:

On converting Central Time to Eastern Standard Time (which is one hour later) you find that one o'clock Central Time is equivalent to two o'clock Eastern Standard Time.

Glancing at the time chart you see you must add six hours to your Eastern Time figure, which means it is eight o'clock in Le Havre. Now you know that it is improbable that anyone would be in the office at this hour to receive a cablegram. This means you can use the letter telegram and cut the cost in half, and you can send a longer message.

HOW TO COMPUTE CABLE CHARGES. The best way to save money is to learn how the service assesses charges, and act accordingly. Words in cablegrams cost more than words in telegrams because of the greater distance they travel. Each additional word will add to your costs but there are ways to keep the count to a minimum.

To determine STANDARD TIME overseas
add (+) to or subtract (—) from
EASTERN STANDARD TIME as indicated:

Afghanistan	+	9½	Belgium	+	6
Albania	+	6	Bermuda	+	1
Algeria	+	6	Bolivia	+	1
Argentina	+	2	Borneo	+	13
Aruba	+	½	Brazil	+	2 (2)*
Australia	+	15 (1)*	Bulgaria	+	7
Austria	+	6	Burma	+	11½
Azores	+	3	Canal Zone		0

Ceylon	+	10½		Madagascar	+	8	
Chile	+	1		Malaya	+	12½	
China	+	13	(3)*	Morocco	+	5	
Colombia		0		Netherlands	+	6	
Congo, Rep of	+	6	(4)*	Neth Antilles	+	½	
Costa Rica	—	1		Newfoundland	+	1½	
Cuba		0		New Zealand	+	17	
Curacao	+	½		Nicaragua	—	1	
Czechoslovakia	+	6		Norway	+	6	
Denmark	+	6		Pakistan	+	10	(6)*
Dominican Rep		0		Panama		0	
Ecuador		0		Paraguay	+	1	
Egypt	+	7		Peru		0	
Ethiopia	+	8		Philippines	+	13	
Finland	+	7		Poland	+	6	(7)*
Formosa	+	13		Portugal	+	5	
France	+	6		Puerto Rico	+	1	
Germany	+	6		Rhodesia	+	7	
Ghana	+	5		Roumania	+	7	
Great Britain	+	5		Salvador (El)	—	1	
Greece	+	7		Saudi Arabia	+	8	(8)*
Guatemala	—	1		Singapore	+	12½	
Haiti		0		Spain	+	6	
Hawaii	—	5		Surinam	+	1½	
Hungary	+	6		Sweden	+	6	
Iceland	+	4		Switzerland	+	6	
India	+	10½		Syria	+	7	
Indonesia	+	12½	(5)*	Thailand	+	12	
Iran	+	8½		Tunisia	+	6	
Iraq	+	8		Turkey	+	7	
Ireland	+	5		Union S Africa	+	7	
Israel	+	7		U S S R	+	8	(9)*
Italy	+	6		Uruguay	+	2	
Japan	+	14		Venezuela	+	½	
Korea	+	13½		Viet-Nam	+	12	
Lebanon	+	7		Virgin Islands	+	1	
Luxembourg	+	6		Yugoslavia	+	6	

Note: (1)* Brisbane, Canberra, Melbourne, New So. Wales, Sydney, Queensland.

(2)* Rio de Janeiro, Sao Paulo, Santos.

(3)* Hong Kong, Peiping, Shanghai, Tientsin.

(4)* Leopoldville.

(5)* Djakarta.

(6)* Karachi.

(7)* Warsaw.

(8)* Djeddah.

(9)* Moscow.

Addresses. The name of the place or destination, including the country, when it is necessary for identification, is counted as one word regardless of the number of letters it contains. You may run together the names of persons and streets to the count of fifteen or any fraction thereof and it will count as one word. CHAMPSELYSEES is one word but CHAMPS ELYSEES is two words. You may also use registered code addresses.

Signature and address of senders. You will be charged by the word here, but you need not sign the cable or you may sign it with a code signature.

Plain-language messages. When words are 15 letters or less they are counted as one word each. Words with more than 15 letters are counted at the rate of fifteen letters to the word.

Code messages. When messages are sent in secret (code or cipher) language, they are assessed at the rate of five characters or fraction thereof to the word.

Mixed groups of letters and figures. Groups of figures, or of figures and words, are counted at the rate of five, or fraction thereof, to the word. Counting as separate words are dollar and cent signs and pound sterling marks. However, fraction bars, commas, and decimal points may be grouped with the figures and letters. In this fashion they would count as one character in the group of which they are a part. Therefore, 3,565,320.78, or 76/7 are counted as one word each, but $89.50 and 57¢ are counted as two words each.

Abbreviations. FOB, CIF and other commercial marks and abbreviations are permitted and counted at the rate of five letters to each word. You may not use abbreviations contrary to common usage.

Punctuation marks. Unless you place a specific request, punctuation marks, hyphens and apostrophes will not be transmitted. When they are used, they are charged at the rate of one word each.

Report of delivery. Type "PC" for a telegraph report or "PCP" (for a postal card report) immediately before the address when you want notification of the date and time of delivery. One-half the full-rate toll is charged for this service.

Messages repeated back. You may have a message repeated back to you if you type the chargeable service indication "TC" immediately before the address. The charge for this service is computed by adding the rate for one word to full-rate toll and multiplying this sum by one and one-half.

Prepaid replies. If you wish to indicate to the cable people that you are willing to prepay a reply, type "RP" and follow with the amount prepaid. The indication should be placed immediately before, and as part of, the address, and carries a charge as for one word.

Fee for prepayment is charged or collected at the time the message is accepted, whether or not a reply is actually made. The telegraph follows this practice as they must remit the money through their international accounts to the office of destination.

Registered code addresses. You already know that charges are assessed on each word in addresses and signatures on wires sent to other countries. This expense is curtailed by several firms who have registered a one word code address and signature. These may be employed in all international cablegrams and radiograms.

A code address can be arranged by contacting either the Central Bureau of Registered Addresses, 67 Broad Street, New York; international carriers maintaining offices at Washington, D. C. (American Cable and Radio and RCA Communications) and at San Francisco (American Cable and Radio, RCA Communications, and Globe Wireless); or with any Western Union office. You only need to register the address with one office in each city, which then supplies the local office of other carriers with each new registration. There is a registration fee of $15.00 a year, or $9.00 for six months when you register a code address.

WHAT IS THE "BLUE BOOK"? You will remember that we mentioned you have a choice of carriers when you send radiograms and cablegrams. This choice is important, since not all carriers have offices in every major city in the world. Rates are comparable and all carriers get their messages through, but there may be one carrier with a direct link to the city you want. You want to avoid circuitous routings which waste time so you will check the *"Factual Analysis of Principal International Telegraph Routes."* This is the "Blue Book" of the trade. It is distributed by The American Cable & Radio Corporation without cost, and also shows the best ways to send your messages overseas. It contains an alphabetical listing of countries plus additional information on rates, time zones, bank holidays, local currency, and other useful data.

A simple request to The American Cable & Radio Corporation in New York will bring you a copy of the "Blue Book."

► **Summary**. Review this check list before you send a telegram or cable:

1. Check to see how important the speed factor will be.
2. Check time zones.
3. Check the most economical classification for your message.

4. Check the wording of your message. Is it clear and concise without any unnecessary words to add to the cost?
5. Check the rules for computing costs. See where you can consolidate for greater economy.

7. HOW TO INSURE THAT YOU FOLLOW INSTRUCTIONS FAITHFULLY

A secretary's job is to follow instructions. When your employer asks you to do something, he wants to feel confident that you will carry out his wishes to the letter. You must start building your reputation for reliability from your first day on the job—and you can.

This section tells you what to do so you won't "forget to remember."

PUT IT IN WRITING AND DON'T BE AFRAID TO ASK QUESTIONS. The secret of following instructions exactly and not forgetting important things, no matter how busy you are, is very simple: don't rely on your memory. Instead, use written reminder systems that won't let you forget. It's easier on your brain and on your nerves; you worry less and are more efficient.

For example, when your executive calls you into his office and spells out something he wants done, his instructions may seem quite clear. Even so, take a few seconds to jot down the assignment in shorthand; you'll avoid being plagued by doubts later on because you feel you have omitted something vital.

Don't be afraid to ask questions when you don't understand instructions. Any employer would much rather take a few extra seconds to explain his instructions and have the job done right than be kept waiting a half hour while you do it all over again.

MAINTAIN A CALENDAR. Every secretary should keep an accurate and thorough record of up-coming events (appointments, meetings, deadlines, and so on). Even if you never forget such things, its dangerous to keep schedules in your head; what happens when you are out ill?

Experienced secretaries have found that the best system for keeping track of coming events is to enter everything on calendars. Here's how that works.

A calendar for yourself. Obtain a standard desk calendar pad, or use a yearbook-type calendar. You will probably find the desk pad most helpful as it is in full view all of the time. For added convenience, try to get a calendar pad with 15-minute or 30-minute time divisions.

Your calendar should carry the following notations:

1. Your own activities and business appointments, with reminders noted a day or two before.
2. Your employer's appointments and all other items that you generally bring to his attention, with reminders noted a day or two before.
3. Reminders on jobs that must be completed by a certain date.

A calendar for your employer. Again, the standard desk calendar pad or yearbook will serve the purpose nicely, although your executive may prefer a yearbook in order to keep the contents away from the eyes of prying callers. The primary purpose of this calendar is to keep a record of your employer's appointments. Therefore, the pages must be large enough so you can note the other party's affiliation along with his name.

This calendar also serves to remind your employer of important personal dates, such as his wife's birthday, his wedding anniversary, and his children's birthdays. It is not necessary to note the dates beforehand as you did on your own calendar. Check from time to time to make sure that your employer has not made any appointments that he forgot to tell you about.

A pocket memo calendar. Here is where you note all the engagements that might conflict with future appointments that your employer himself makes. Your employer will carry this book with him to luncheons and meetings so he can schedule appointments without worrying about whether he has any other meetings at that time.

HAVE A TICKLER FILE. One of the handiest systems you can employ is a tickler card file to be used in conjunction with your calendars. A card tickler file has a tabbed guide for each month of the year and 31 tabbed guides, one for each day of the current month. The daily guides are placed behind the current month guide. Memoranda are made on cards, and the cards are filed behind the daily guide according to the date on which the matter is to be brought up.

Information to be placed on the cards may include:

Holidays—With notations where presents or cards are normally sent
Business meetings
Payment dates—Loans, Insurance, Charity Pledges, etc.
Renewal dates—Subscriptions, Automobile License
Tax dates—Federal, State, Local

As you learn of a meeting or a payment date, type all the necessary information on a card and file it under the appropriate date.

When you have an item that occurs more than once during the year, make out one card and move it up from month to month. For example, let's say your employer pays an insurance premium four times a year. After the first payment, move the card up to the date for the next payment, and so on.

As you can see, this system saves you considerable work in preparing your calendars. Give your card file and your calendar a quick check every morning.

► **Warning.** The card system is not a substitute for your calendars where *appointments* are concerned. If you try to make it one, you will find yourself consulting calendars and cards every time you have to make an appointment for your employer. Keep your records of business appointments on the calendars.

WAYS OF REMINDING YOUR EMPLOYER. Each morning, give your employer a typed list of his appointments for the day. Be sure to include the caller's affiliation and the reason for the visit. Just before it is time for each meeting, give your employer any written data or file that concerns his business with the caller.

When your employer asks you to remind him to act on a certain matter, make a notation on your calendar. When the time comes, place the proper file on his desk, with a note stating what he wanted to do.

For instance: Your boss may say "I want to send a letter out to Johnson, if we don't have his report on Friday." You put a note on your calendar—"Letter to Johnson if report not in." On Friday place any written material you have concerning the report on your employer's desk with the note—"You wanted to send a letter to Mr. Johnson, if his report wasn't in today."

KEEP A CONTACT FILE. You and your employer will be continually making new contacts. Whenever you are introduced to a new business contact, get the correct spelling of his name, write it down (including hints on pronunciation if the name is unusual), and file it for future reference. This file can be kept in card form or in a loose-leaf binder.

If your employer makes a lot of new contacts, he will appreciate having a reminder file on hand. Explain the file to your boss and get him in the habit of telling you pertinent facts about people so you can keep the entries up to date. When you place a name in the file, include the company affiliation and the circumstances of the meeting. Future clients are always favorably impressed when an executive remembers their name and company after just one introduction.

► **Summary**

Want to be sure you are following instructions?

1. Ask questions when you don't understand.
2. Concentrate on what you are doing.
3. Learn to ignore petty annoyances.
4. Maintain a positive attitude toward your work.

Want to be sure you won't "forget to remember?"

1. Put it in writing.
2. Maintain a calendar.
3. Start a reminder system.

8. SHOULD YOU GUESS RATHER THAN TAKE TIME TO "LOOK IT UP?"

When you are very busy, are you tempted to guess when you are not certain of something, rather than take the time to look it up? Many secretaries yield to this temptation, but the odds are definitely against them when they do. After all, the man you work for has every right to expect accurate work. If there is fact or information connected with your work that you don't know, he expects you to be able to find it, and he counts on you to do so.

This section gives you some tips on where you can quickly lay your hands on information you might need during the course of a day in a typical office. The important thing is to *use* sources of information; look it up, don't guess.

FOUR PRIMARY SOURCES OF INFORMATION. Here are four basic reference books you should have on your desk or near at hand. They include a dictionary, Thesaurus, almanac, and telephone directory. Here is a rundown on what you can find in each.

Dictionary. This book was not meant to be just a paperweight; on the contrary, it can be the handiest book in your office. A dictionary gives you the following information (and more) on a troublesome word:

How you spell it (and how you spell plural, and possessive forms).
Where you can break it at the end of a line.
What it means.
What part of speech it is.
Words that mean the same or the opposite.

When you are looking up a word, you may find that it has two acceptable spellings. Unless you have an office style guide which includes preferred spellings, use the first spelling found in the dictionary.

Get in the habit of checking with your dictionary when you are in doubt about how to spell a word or how to hyphenate it at the end of a line.

Telephone Directory. In addition to giving you addresses and telephone numbers, your telephone directory also shows you the correct spelling of firm names. When you are writing to a potential client for the first time, it makes a very poor impression to misspell his name, or his company's name. Consult your telephone directory as you would your dictionary.

Another important source of information is the Yellow Pages. Through the Yellow Pages, you can locate car rental agencies, employment agencies for permanent or temporary help, travel agencies, sources of office equipment and supplies, and so on. For example, if you should need a dictating machine repairman, you would simply look in the Yellow Pages under Office Equipment or Dictating Machines and find an advertisement for your make that says "Sales and Service."

Thesaurus. Do you know what you want to say but can't quite find the right words? Can you phrase the main thought in a letter in more than one way so you don't repeat yourself? You can solve these problems with a Thesaurus, which provides you with synonyms for words in the English language. Let us say you are seeking a synonym for "obligatory." You look up the word you wish to replace in the second half of the Thesaurus, which is compiled alphabetically. This is the way it would appear:

obligatory

necessary 637.12
mandatory 750.13
compulsory 754.9
incumbent upon 960.14[1]

Now assume that "mandatory" is closest to the meaning you want to express. Go to the first half of the book, which is set up numerically from 1 to 1040. Turn to the 700 section, find 750, and look under part 13. There you will see:

750.13

ADJS. 13. **mandatory, imperative, commanding, compulsory,** peremptory, **obligatory,** must; decisive, final, conclusive, binding, irrevocable, without appeal.[2]

---

[1]From "ROGET'S INTERNATIONAL THESAURUS," Third Edition, copyright © 1962 by Thomas Y. Crowell Company, New York, publishers.
[2]Ibid.

The number 756 gives you a further reference if you still haven't found a suitable synonym.

When you catch yourself repeating words, phrases, or constructions in your letters and reports, reach for your Thesaurus.

Almanac. Do you have to address a letter to your employer's representative in Congress, or to the mayor of another city? Does your employer want statistics on American economical growth for the past year? If you have a current almanac, the answers are already at your fingertips. Usually priced under two dollars, almanacs contain a wealth of current and historical information. A few of the headings generally included are:

Top News Stories of the Year in Chronological Order
Government Officials—State and Federal
Maps of the World
History of Presidential Elections
Famous People in Art, Science and Literature
Sports News
Statistics on the American Economy
Statistics on Education
Statistics on Religion
Geography of the World
History of the World by Country

An almanac is a relatively small investment which can pay big dividends in time saved.

SOME OTHER SOURCES YOU MAY HAVE OCCASION TO USE. Here are four more sources that can be very helpful when you need information. Unlike the ones just mentioned, these might require a trip to your company or community library.

Of course, these are only examples of especially helpful sources for the secretary; there are many more, you will find, at any library.

1. Moody's Manuals: Is your employer looking for the financial statements of the Jones Company? Does he want to know who is on their board of directors? You can find the answers quickly and easily in one of *Moody's Manuals.* Most libraries carry a complete set in their reference section. The manuals cover industrial, transportation, public utility, bank and finance companies. They also contain highlights of outstanding bond and stock issues. (There are other, similar sources; *Thomas' Register of American Manufacturers* is one, for example.)

2. Official Register of the U.S. Government: Have to know "Who's Who" in Washington? Here's the book with the answers. It lists all persons holding administrative or supervisory positions in the legislative, executive, and judicial branches of the Federal government and the District of Columbia. The publication appears practically annually and gives the person's name, title, legal residence, and in most cases, salary. Indexing is by name and by agency. You can find this volume in most libraries.

3. New York Times Index: Suppose your employer wants the text of a speech made at the United Nations last month by a visiting diplomat, or wants to know when a certain event took place. A good place to check is the *New York Times Index.* This is an index of the contents of this newspaper. It is published frequently, with a final cumulative index for each year. Reference is given to the date of the paper, page number and column number. Most libraries have this index in their reference section. The index is particularly helpful when you are looking up an obituary, the full text of a speech or document, or book or theater reviews.

4. How and Where to Look It Up (by Robert Murphey; McGraw-Hill): Don't even know where to start looking for an answer? This volume is one of your best guides to all sources of information; it tells you where to find the data you are seeking. A secretary who does a great deal of research will find it most valuable. Again, your library probably has a copy in their reference section.

► **Tip.** When you need an odd piece of information right away, and it isn't available in one of your desk books, you might try calling your local newspaper. Some of the larger papers have regular information services which operate free of charge. Check the papers in your area today so you will know which one to call in an emergency. Sometimes your library will give information over the phone, too.

Once you know where to look up information, and make a habit of checking, you will avoid careless mistakes. Remember, a professional secretary *never* guesses; she looks it up.